HAUNTED
SOUTHERN
CALIFORNIA

HAUNTED SOUTHERN CALIFORNIA

BRIAN CLUNE

Haunted
america

Published by Haunted America,
A Division of The History Press
Charleston, SC
www.historypress.com

Unless otherwise noted, images are courtesy of Terri Clune.

First published 2022

Manufactured in the United States

ISBN 9781467152433

Library of Congress Control Number: 2022937942

Southern California is known for its sun, beaches and pleasure piers.

This book is dedicated to all of the folks who selflessly work to keep the wonderful history of the Golden State alive through their efforts of preservation and care of the locations they serve. I also dedicate this to the woman who can do magic and keeps me going just by being here and being my muse.
I hope your magic lives within me, always.

Outside, in the world, people struck each other, yelled and honked horns.
Inside, in the theater, they conversed by singing and dancing.
I knew that is where I belonged.

—Marta Becket, owner of the Amargosa Hotel and Opera House

CONTENTS

CONTENTS

FOREWORD

When I was a small child, I remember being called the "strange kid" since I liked going to the library and looking for books about ghosts and haunted places. When you're young, all you can do is read the stories and just imagine what it would be like to be there. Tales of spirits and specters haunting the homes and historical landmarks we know capture our minds. I looked for many places to go explore and chase the shadows along with local urban legends in our town and always thought about other towns and their legends as well.

I have known the author, Brian Clune, for a while now and he has always had a passion for history and has been great about putting forth information on locations along with deep details about hidden history. He has a natural ability to get to the heart of the stories and can get a personal view from the people he interviews regarding the places he writes about.

I have been investigating for over thirty years, and there were so many times I had to look and hunt to find the places that I would want to investigate. Brian has now put together a bucket list of many places that would have taken us years to discover on our own. Now we can just pick the books that he has compiled for different areas, and we can travel to and create our own haunted expeditions.

Honestly, I wish there were books and information like Brian's in my days perusing the school library. We now have the history and the names of the people involved in the locations. As an investigator, it helps us in asking the proper questions to the spirits who were born, lived and passed in these places. With all the knowledge Brian has provided in these books, I truly believe that investigators and historical explorers will use these books for many generations to come.

Brian, please continue bringing us the haunted history, and thank you for all the work you have done.

—Stefan Brigati, host of *My Darkest Hour* podcast,
co-host of No Cover Radio and manager of
the haunted Majestic Theater in Ventura, California

Acknowledgements

There are people I need to thank for helping me with this book, so many it would fill a book all of its own. I would like to thank my acquisitions editor, Laurie Krill, once again for all of her hard work. You will never know how much it means to me. A big thank-you goes out to my friend Louis Montero for going along with me on a few adventures required to complete this book and going through picture hell trying to get me some photos for one of the locations. Thank you to Heather Raymond-Huerta, who was kind enough to give me a personal tour of and read the chapter about the Zalud House, to make sure I had the history correct. Willie Flores, manager of the Mayan Bar and Grill at the Aztec Hotel, has my profound thanks for giving me access to the property for my research, as well as the entire staff for their kindness. I want to thank my wife, Terri, and my kids for their support and belief in me, and finally, I need to thank my readers. If it wasn't for you, I would still be writing only personal journals. Thank you all from the bottom of my heart.

Introduction
Southern California, Movie Stars, Beaches, Sun and Spirits

When folks around the country think about Southern California, the first things that usually come to mind are beaches, Hollywood, Disneyland and perpetual sunshine. Much of this comes from the early days of Hollywood glitz, glamour and movies that showed only the sunny side of SoCal. When Walt Disney Studios came into being, the fun and lovable characters in its animated movies helped solidify this image, and after the now famous Magic Kingdom of Disneyland opened, the rest of the United States, and the world, began to believe that Southern California was the place where dreams come true, the sun was never obscured by clouds and happiness was around every corner.

Much like Hollywood itself, the image of Southern California is nothing more than wishes, dreams and a hope that whatever one wants in life is theirs for the taking, if only they head to the ever-sunny Pacific coast. However, just like the movies, there are things unseen that the sunshine is wont to hide and keeps from an unsuspecting viewer until the proper time it needs to be revealed. If you look just beneath the surface and examine the history of California, you will see a state plagued with hardships, conquest, murder and proselytizing that did its best to darken the dream of California's birth. Even places where fun and gaiety are known factors, you will find hidden stories that can chill one to the bone and make even the staunchest human afraid to close their eyes and go to sleep.

Behind the sun, and beneath the sandy beaches lies a much darker and sordid history, a history that many don't know or want to know. Murders,

Do Sharon Tate and the others killed on this property still walk the halls of the new mansion?

betrayal, suicide and witches all helped shape Southern California into what it is today: a place of lost dreams turned into nightmares and wandering spirits looking for succor and release from their unfinished business. From oceangoing vessels, amusement parks and even churches, these spirits are always with us, always seeking us out, wanting answers to their plight and help passing through the veil into the loving arms of eternity.

Read on if you dare, and delve deeper into the abyss of darkness that is the realm of death. Look to these pages for tales of love gone bad and greed turned deadly. Find devotion in the words of those who refuse to pass on for the love of art or love that they thought was theirs, only to discover it was unrequited. In these pages, you will find the darker side of Southern California. But even as night turns into the light of day, so can the spirit realm turn to the light of salvation and peace if one only looks.

Southern California, sunshine, beaches, movie stars and spirits. It can all be found here in abundance if one only looks. It is a ParaTraveler's dream where adventure awaits, so enjoy the journey as you explore all of the wonders SoCal has to offer.

1

THE SANTA MARIA INN

When Frank McCoy arrived in Santa Maria, California, in 1904, it was to begin work for Union Sugar, the main industry in Santa Maria at that time. McCoy had dreams of becoming a hotelier, and it wasn't long before he made that dream come true. In 1917, McCoy built the Santa Maria Inn. When opened, this hotel was one of the most modern buildings in California and—with each of the twenty-four guest rooms containing its own private bathroom—one of the most unusual and luxurious. Because of the grand accommodations, the Santa Maria Inn began to draw a lot of high-class and important guests. Movie stars such as Charlie Chaplin, Mary Pickford and Bob Hope became regulars. Dignitaries and others visiting William Randolph Hearst's castle for the newspaperman's legendary parties in nearby San Simeon would make the hotel their go-to place to stay and recover.

Over the years, rooms were added to accommodate the growing number of guests passing through and needing a place to stay. In 1930, another sixty-one rooms were added, bringing the total to eighty-five, and in 1941, twenty-two motel rooms and a swimming pool were added. Then, in 1981, after a complete renovation, the Santa Maria Inn reopened, this time with an added six-story modern building. This new addition provided five new floors of guest rooms, with the first floor being leased for local business offices. The original inn underwent extensive renovations as well, bringing the old wing into the twentieth century without sacrificing any of the old-world charm.

The Santa Maria Inn has gone through many changes since its humble beginning.

The rooms that were known to host celebrities of the past were each given a star on the outside of the door, with the celebrity's name prominently displayed within the star. It would seem that this honor has pleased many of those stars, including long-deceased Rudolph Valentino. Valentino, who spent quite a bit of time at the Santa Maria Inn, has decided that the hotel is still the place he wants to vacation, even in the afterlife.

Legendary heartthrob Rudolph Valentino visited the Santa Maria Inn more than once and is known to haunt the room where he stayed, which has a star with his name on the outside of the door. Many of those who have stayed in room 221 claimed to have heard and seen him. Those guests who check into the room without knowing its history will call down to the front desk to ask them to send someone up to stop whoever is pranking them by knocking on the door. They don't realize that is one of the things for which Valentino is best known, knocking on the door to "his" room. Many guests have told the staff about hearing a knock on the door, and when opened, no one is there. Often, just as they close the door, the knock will sound again, and even though they immediately reopen the door, again, no one is present. The front desk now makes sure to mention this phenomenon when guests check in.

Another common occurrence in room 221 is seeing what looks like a figure lying down in the bed, even though the bed had been made, yet no one can be seen. There have been times when a guest will be looking at the bed and actually see the bed move as if someone sat down on the edge and then lay down. The bed will actually indent, as will the pillows as if a head had just been placed there to take a nap. Needless to say, this can be a bit alarming for those who may not have heard about the spirit. There have been times, albeit rare, when Valentino has been seen standing by the bed, as if watching the guests sleep, or sitting in one of the chairs in the room.

Another spirit that calls the hotel home—one that has been at the Santa Maria Inn almost from the day it opened—is known only as "The Captain." The Captain was first seen a couple of years after the hotel opened, and no one is sure who this man is, but it is rumored that he was murdered by his mistress and this is the reason he haunts the inn. The Captain is seen all over the hotel, and there is no certain time of day or night when he may appear, but he seems to be mainly attached to room 210. Regardless of which room the Captain seems to prefer, he also likes to wander. According to the staff at the hotel, during renovations, a couple staying on the first floor of the old section of the inn reported hearing footsteps going up and down the hallway for a couple of hours. Thinking it was the workers, they didn't pay close attention to it, but when they exited their room, saw that there was no one in the hall and still heard the sounds, they began to realize what was going on. Later that night, the couple kept hearing doors opening and closing and again, upon inspection, found no one in the halls as the sound continued. After hearing about the Captain, they believe he may have been having some fun with them.

It isn't just guests who have seen the Captain or his handiwork. Just after reopening, one of the inn's gardeners saw the image of a man standing on one of the outside stairwell landings. He was about to ask the guest if he

could help in any way when the man simply vanished from sight, never moving. The gardener was white as a ghost as he walked up to the front desk to let them know he had just seen the Captain. One of the managers has said that in room 216, the curtains will suddenly billow even though the windows are shut and locked and there is no noticeable breeze wafting through.

There is one other known spirit that resides at the inn, and she is supposedly that of a cocaine addict by the name of Peppy. It's said that she

Rudolph Valentino stayed here many times, and still considers this room as his own.

Above: The hands of clocks at the hotel, such as this one, will begin to spin wildly for no reason.

Left: Piano music can be heard throughout the hotel even when no one is at the keys.

either got her name from her always upbeat nature or was nicknamed by her aunt. A psychic who visited the Santa Maria Inn years ago claimed to have made contact with Peppy. The spirit said that she traveled to Hearst Castle with her aunt, and they would spend the night at the inn while visiting WR (William Randolph [Hearst]). There is a bit of truth to this tale, as evidence was found that there was a sister of Marion Davies, Hearst's mistress, who may have had a niece by that nickname. An actress by the name of Alma Rubens, who is known to have come to the castle during the same period, did die from an overdose in the 1930s, and some speculate this may be the spirit known as Peppy.

There are other things that happen in and around the hotel, such as lights that all of a sudden develop a pronounced strobe effect, shadows that will briefly follow guests as they make their way down the hallways of the old inn, and clocks whose hands will mysteriously and unexpectedly begin to spin wildly. There is even the sound of a piano that will begin playing on its own accord to serenade startled guests. Strange footprints have been seen in the gardens, and outside doors will suddenly slam shut as folks walk nearby, and reports have come from almost everywhere at the inn, including the cellar.

The Santa Maria Inn gets good reviews on TripAdvisor, as do the ghosts. One guest wrote on the site, "Saw a few 'strange' things happen, like a vending machine working on its own, and a fork and knife appear out of nowhere." Another guest wrote, "It was definitely haunted with old spirits. If you like that sort of thing, by all means, plan a trip here. There were a lot of unidentified creaks, and noises throughout the night…and I was plagued with nightmares." There is even a review that states that the guest stayed in room 210 and had so much activity that he made a YouTube video of all that occurred while he was there.

The Santa Maria Inn, with its long history and resident spirits, is a place every ParaTraveler should stay at least once. Having stayed in room 221 myself, I can at least say that there is a definite vibe at the inn that screams *haunted*. If one needs an excuse to come to Santa Maria and the inn, besides the ghosts of course, it would be for the famous Santa Maria barbecue. Many people around the country and the world claim it is better than Texas, Memphis or any other barbecue. Just make sure when returning from dinner, you bring the leftovers for the spirits. I mean, who doesn't love good barbecue?

2
La Purisima Mission

California missions are not just famous within the state; most people around the world have heard of them. Although other states, such as Arizona, New Mexico and Texas, have their own missions, none has produced the allure and romance that the California mission system seems to have in the minds of Americans in quite the same way. Many folks visiting the missions feel a sense of calm and peacefulness; even those who are not of the Catholic faith or even Christian will find themselves content within the gardens and fields of these old church grounds. What many people don't know is that most of these peaceful bastions of Christianity were founded by brutal tactics and suppression of the Native Americans' own beliefs. Because of these sometimes-deadly methods of conversion, it is not surprising that many missions are haunted, and La Purisima, near Lompoc, California, may be at the top of this list.

Originally founded in 1787, La Purisima was completely destroyed in 1812 by a series of earthquakes that struck the area. The mission was rebuilt using many of the stones and wood beams that were salvaged from the old mission on the opposite side of the Santa Inez River to an area better suited to farming and closer to its water source. That same mission is still there today.

As was mentioned, the Spanish were not always gentle in converting the Native Americans into Christians. Even the padres had a tendency to treat the Chumash Indians more like slaves than converts. In 1824, after having endured forced labor, separation from their families and beatings from the

La Purisima may be the most haunted mission in the California mission system.

mission guards, the Chumash finally rebelled against Mexico, and fighting erupted between Native and Mexican troops. The rebellion was quickly put down, with loss of life on both sides, and since that day, ghosts have been reported on the mission grounds and in the buildings.

Padre Mariano Payeras, the man who directed the entire California mission system from his beloved La Purisima, and one of the most revered priests from the time of the missionaries, passed away on April 23, 1823, and is buried under the altar in the main church. Padre Payeras is one of only a very few to be honored in this way, and it would seem that the good padre was not ready to leave his beloved mission. Father Payeras has been seen standing near where his body is interred, in the full regalia of the priesthood as if he is about to perform Mass for those who are present. One should tread lightly when entering the church, as it is said that those who enter the church with disrespect will be cursed with bad luck until they return to La Purisima and make amends in front of the altar and Father Payeras. There have been times when folks walking past the church have heard the sound of people in prayer, only to find out on entering the church that there is no one inside and all of the praying has ceased. There are even reports from folks who have heard the sound of singing coming from the church, as if Mass is in full swing, but again, when they enter the church, there is no one

Padre Payeras is buried under the altar at La Purisima, and he is said to haunt the entire mission.

there and the singing has vanished. In the sacristy behind the altar, folks will walk in to find a priest preparing for Mass. With apologies, visitors will turn to leave; the padre will stop what he is doing to look, simply smile and fade from view. No one is sure which padre this is, but it is believed to be Payeras, still tending to his flock.

Father Payeras is seen not only in the sacristy and church but also walking along the hallways of the living quarters. When glimpsed, Payeras is described as old and wearing white or black monk's robes. The priest may also be responsible for the bedding in one of the rooms being mussed up each morning when the rangers open up for the day. The room in question had been used as the padre's bedroom over the years and was also sometimes used as a guest room. Many of the rangers and docents at La Purisima have found when they are opening the mission for the day, as they walk through the room, they will find that the bed looks as if it had been slept in. Each day, they make up the bed, walk their rounds while keeping an eye on the room throughout the day, then lock up in the evening, and they still find the bed once again in disarray the following morning. This bed is an original rope-strung bed and hasn't been tightened in many years, so anyone trying to use it to sleep would most likely fall right to the floor. Sleeping "tight," as the saying goes, is not possible on this bed.

The kitchens at the mission are also said to be haunted. The spirit here is believed to be that of Don Vincente, who was murdered on the grounds in the 1820s.

The buildings are not the only places the ParaTraveler will find ghosts at La Purisima Mission. The cemetery and the grounds themselves are also said to be quite haunted. Strange shapes are often seen wandering around in the mission graveyard, and many believe these to be the spirits of those killed or executed after the Chumash uprising. Others believe that the misdeeds of the padres, along with the Mexican and Spanish soldiers, have caused shadow people to inhabit the cemetery. Whether it is soldier, priest or Native American, one should keep a sharp eye out while visiting the cemetery. The grounds of the mission itself seem to be filled with paranormal activity. Many folks visiting the mission have heard the sound of flute music coming from the area near the chapel and baptismal font, as well as from the area where the Chumash used to gather for their tribal festivals and celebrations. Many times, the flute music will be accompanied by the sound of drums. The drums will begin as a faint staccato and slowly begin to build to a crescendo. When the music finally reaches its peak, the voices of people chanting begins, and the sounds of dancing will follow. In one amazing tale,

Almost every morning, this rope-strung bed looks as if it had been slept in during the night.

a visitor ran to the park ranger's office with a story that she had seen a group of Native Americans appear before her and her kids, dancing in front of a giant bonfire. The woman said that those they watched dance had been transparent and were gone as quickly as they had appeared.

As dramatic as this story seems, most activity at La Purisima Mission is much less exciting. Typical of most haunted locations, cold spots pop up all over the grounds and buildings even when the temperatures outside are high. Male voices can oftentimes be heard when no one is near, and the sound of horses clopping along the old road directly in front of the buildings are often noticeable even though horses are nowhere to be found. There have even been reports of spectral dogs who have been spotted walking along as if they are led on a leash, held by folks who cannot be seen. From long-deceased Spanish and Mexican soldiers still guarding the mission jail and patrolling the grounds to phantom voices heard within the church, kitchens and living quarters, La Purisima is one place the intrepid ParaTraveler should make it their mission in life to visit.

3

ZALUD HOUSE

ohn Zalud immigrated to the United States from Bohemia while in his youth. Living among other folks from his homeland, John fell in love with and married fellow Bohemian Mary Herdicka in the city of San Francisco in 1875. Shortly thereafter, the Zaluds moved to the town of Tulare and became some of the earliest settlers to the San Joaquin Valley. Once situated in town, John opened a restaurant named Delmonico's, meant to serve the many railroad employees who worked in the large railyard in Tulare. However, by 1890 the railyards were shutting down and Zalud's business was failing. John and Mary decided to move their family northeast to the town of Porterville, California. Here, John established a saloon and, some say, gambling house on Main Street. Zalud made enough money to make some smart real estate investments, and when those paid off, he bought some property on Hockett Street. John had a fine house built, and by late 1891, John, Mary and their three children had moved into what became known as the Zalud House.

The family lived in the house for many years with few problems, but in one tragic incident, the Zaluds lost their youngest child, Inez, at the age of three months; however, all in all, life seemed to be going quite well for them all. Pearle, their second-youngest child, graduated from high school and attended the New England Conservatory of Music. This was one of the most prestigious music schools in the country. Her time in Boston may have sparked her later love of travel. When Pearle returned to Porterville, along with her exquisite skill on the piano, she began to give piano lessons and

The Zalud House may be the most haunted location in California's Central Valley.

made a good living doing so. Unfortunately, as life is wont to do, it started putting roadblocks in the way of the Zalud family.

In 1912, Mary Zalud passed away, and that seems to have started a series of misfortunes for the family. Five years after Mary's death, Annie Zalud's husband was murdered in a bizarre event that would have a lasting effect on the Zalud House, and then five years after this murder, Edward Zalud was killed in an accident on his horse. His horse stepped on a squirrel, which caused Edward to fall, and he was then kicked in the head by his horse; he never regained consciousness after the fall. There were rumors circulating at the time that Edward may have been caught cattle rustling and became the victim of "frontier justice," vigilantism. Other rumors claim that Edward was a bootlegger and may have been ambushed by rival liquor runners. This may come from an earlier incident when he was caught illegally selling booze to the local Native Americans. Edward never spent time in jail for this; however, he was fined fifty dollars.

After the murder of Annie's husband, followed by the death of Edward, John, Annie and Pearle took their first world cruise in 1924 around the globe. The three Zaluds spent a lot of time traveling the world and enjoying one another's company. John Zalud and Pearle lived with Annie in her home in downtown Los Angeles. This is where Annie and her husband, Will, would initially live after leaving the San Francisco area around 1906. Pearle, it would seem, enjoyed shopping on these excursions, and quite a few things she picked up along the way are still in the Zalud House Museum today. John Zalud passed away in 1944, and after his death, Pearle continued to travel back and forth. After the death of Annie in 1962, Pearle remained in Porterville and lived in her family home until she passed away in 1970.

Pearle never married, although a close friend of the family said that she had once been engaged but never married. Her fiancé, Alex, developed gangrene and passed away. After this, Pearle always considered herself to be a widow. As such, when Pearle died, her only remaining family were cousins, and this is one reason why she left the home and all its possessions to the City of Porterville in her will. Along with the house, Pearle also donated fifteen acres of land to the city, with the stipulation that it be turned into a park for the children and citizens of Porterville. That park still welcomes kids, sports fans and lovers to its peaceful and pristine surroundings. Pearle also left about three thousand acres to various youth groups, including FFA (Future Farmers of America) and the Catholic Diocese of Fresno.

The Zalud House is now a museum run and overseen by the city. It is one of the most unusual museums in the country, as it was lived in by only one family for its entire existence, is furnished by that family's own furniture and has never needed or ever had major changes or renovations. It is still one of the only homes of its kind in the area, being of Second Empire style with a mansard (steep slope) roof and fine wood detailing. Also unusual is the fact that the home was constructed of brick, rather than wood, which was favored for the style. Since opening as a museum, the Zalud House hosts around six thousand guests a year who tour the home, and that number doesn't include those ParaTravelers who come to investigate the many spirits said to inhabit this marvelous piece of Porterville history. For you see, the Zalud House may be the most haunted place in the entire town.

Over the years the museum has welcomed guests to the house, folks have been reporting strange things going on in the old home. Footsteps, strange noises and even stranger feelings will come over the unsuspecting as they tour the house. Even a police officer reported something he couldn't explain. The officer had been sitting in his car out in front of the Zalud House around 2:00 a.m. when suddenly he noticed that all of the lights in the museum turned on. Walking around the house, he didn't see any signs of a break-in and called dispatch to send out a city worker with keys to make sure there were no electrical problems with the house. By the time the municipal employee arrived, the officer said that the lights had simply turned off a few minutes before the worker arrived. Upon inspection, it was found that there was no one inside the museum, and no electrical problems could be found. To this day, neither the officer nor the city worker can explain what happened that night.

One of the things that have been reported has to do with the room where the mother passed away. Many folks who tour the home will walk into this bedroom and become overwhelmed by the feeling of not being able to breathe. Some have said it was as if an asthma attack has hit them, even when they are not afflicted by the disease. People say that their chest gets heavy, followed by not being able to take a deep breath, and then feeling as if they are going to pass out. As soon as they leave the room, all symptoms are gone as if they had never happened. Many folks have refused to go back into or even near that room again.

Another common occurrence within the museum comes from the family dining room. Here, folks have reported smelling the faint aroma of food cooking. The kitchen has gone unused since Pearle passed away, and even though this area was the dining room, no food is allowed in the house. It has been said that footsteps can be heard coming from the kitchen, and as the steps get closer, the aroma gets stronger. It has also been reported that the lights in this room will begin to flicker, and then as suddenly as the flickering began, it will stop. The wires and fixtures have been checked, and nothing can be found to explain this odd flickering.

Perhaps the strangest and scariest stories that involve the Zalud House come from a piece of furniture. Although it did not belong to the Zalud family, it is inextricably linked to them through murder and death. John and Mary's oldest daughter, Annie, was married to a man by the name of William Brooks. William worked for National Cash Register Company (NCR) and was well known not only around town but throughout the state, country and Europe as well due to his tenure at NCR. One of Brooks's longtime friends and co-worker at NCR was one W.C. Howe. Howe lived in Oakland, California, so when William and Annie's San Francisco home was destroyed in the 1906 earthquake that devastated the city, William moved in with his friend, while Annie traveled to Chicago to visit family and then back to Porterville to visit her parents at home. Bill Howe had been recently married to a woman by the name of Orleans, and as she was still getting to know her husband on a deeper level, Brooks would play with her by saying he had a few juicy stories about her husband she might be interested in hearing. When she asked about these stories, all he would say was, "Well, one of these days we will go have lunch and I'll tell you all about him."

William Brooks was murdered in this chair. It is said that William's spirit is still connected to it and now resides at the Zalud House.

Orleans took William Brooks up on his offer and arranged for William to accompany her to San Francisco, where she had an art class, and then go to lunch while in town. Bill Howe knew all about the trip, and as Brooks and Howe were good friends from childhood, he thought nothing about it. The next day, Brooks drove Orleans into town in his topless car. Along the way, Orleans complained about how messy her hair was becoming in the wind and asked Brooks to get a private room at the Poodle Lounge so she could fix her hair from the windy drive. William Brooks was a bit hesitant, knowing that the lounge was an upscale establishment where sometimes illicit affairs would take place, but putting apprehension aside, he made the reservation.

Even though it was a completely innocent talk, where William and Orleans spoke about the funny things her husband had done in his past, and neither was interested in an affair of any kind, some folks who had seen them come into the lounge and enter a private room seemed to get the wrong impression. Even though the lunch was completely innocent in nature, stories began to get around. William made sure to tell his wife, Annie, about the lunch and everything that was talked about, but some people believe that Annie, who understandably no longer trusted Orleans, may have begun a few rumors of her own, although unintentionally. Whatever the truth may be about how the rumors began, they started to have an impact on Howe's marriage. It would all come to a head on November 19, 1917.

Over the years, Orleans found herself ostracized by the other women at NCR, and after finding out about the rumors, she tried to shoot herself in the stomach. Thinking that William was the one spreading rumors about her, Orleans Howe began following William and looking for a way to get him to stop. On November 19, Howe knew that William would be at the Pioneer Hotel in Porterville, went to the hardware store, where she convinced the clerk to sell her a pistol, and then headed over to confront William Brooks. Howe entered the Pioneer Hotel, looked around the room and, seeing Brooks sitting in a chair, turned around and walked back outside. It is not clear why Orleans left the hotel, maybe a moment of lucidity, or fear, but only moments after leaving, she once more turned, entered the hotel and boldly walked up to Brooks, putting four shots into the man, killing him.

After the deed was done, Orleans Howe calmly turned to the men Brooks had been sitting with, handed one of them the gun and said, "A job well done." She then sat down to wait for the police to collect her. Orleans Howe was eventually acquitted of murder on the grounds of mental anguish. In other words, Orleans murdered an innocent man and got away scot-free.

The chair William had been sitting in at the Pioneer Hotel, although never a part of the Zalud House furnishings, is on display in the museum, as it had a severe effect on the family and the family's history. It would seem that William, having been brutally murdered, may have come with the chair back to his wife's childhood home. Over the years the chair has been in the museum, folks have reported severe anxiety just walking into the room, which always seems to get worse as they near the chair. The chair still bears a hole where one of the bullets passed through the body of William Brooks. According to the curator, many folks who have sat in the chair where Brooks was murdered have had chest pains, and a few people report going home afterward to find that they become nauseated and will begin vomiting.

On an episode of the hit television show *Ghost Adventures*, Zak Baggens was told about the chair's unusual ability by the curator's husband, Benny. Benny can channel, and as he and Zak were next to the chair, Benny told Zak to sit down. Zak found out firsthand just what the chair can do to a person. Cast member Aaron, while sitting in the chair, alone in the room, caught a voice responding directly to his queries. It would seem that even skeptics have been convinced by the chair's antics.

The Zalud House has been allowing paranormal investigations since 2008, and reports from some of these are fascinating. It has been confirmed that Pearle, Edward (possibly due to his saddle being in the museum) and of course William Brooks are still in the home. This comes from the many responses that have resulted from recording devices after direct questions had been asked of them. There are two cases that all but prove the family is still looking after their home. One comes from an investigation in which the curator, Heather Raymond-Huerta, was celebrating Mary Jane Zalud's birthday and joked about how many candles it would take on a birthday cake and how much smoke would come once lit. Just after saying this, one of the smoke alarms began to sound. They managed to turn it off, but it seems that Mary Zalud was playing along with the joke about her age.

Another incident occurred when Heather was locking up for the night but couldn't get the alarm to set. After calling the alarm company, the technician told her the company was going to call to reset the alarm and to please not answer the phone when it rang. Heather heard the phone ringing and waited until it stopped, and when she heard her cellphone ring, she figured it was the alarm company telling her everything was reset. When she answered, the woman at the alarm company asked again that she not answer the phone, and when Heather told her she hadn't and that she was the only one in the museum, the alarm technician told her to listen close. The woman once

This is the saddle that Edward Zalud was using when he was thrown from his horse and killed. Could it be keeping him in the house to this day?

again called the museum phone, Heather heard it ring twice and then stop. She then heard over her cellphone a man's voice answer the phone and simply say, "Hello." After a few more tries, the phantom stopped picking up the ringing phone, and they were finally able to reset the alarms.

Other activity in the museum ranges from lights turning on and off for no discernable reason, light fixtures swinging on their own in the kitchen and many direct responses to questions during EVP (electronic voice phenomenon) sessions. There is an old Bohemian clock from the 1860s in the kitchen that uses weights that must be pulled for it to work. These have not been used for a very long time. This clock, on one occasion, began to function even though the weights were still in their neutral position.

It is obvious that the Zalud House is an important piece of not only Porterville history but also the history of California's Central Valley as a whole. As one of the only unaltered house museums left in the country, it is also an important tool for showing folks how people lived, and died, in both the nineteenth and twentieth centuries. As we have seen, it is also a place where every ParaTraveler should come and enjoy. When you visit, make sure you keep in mind that even though long deceased, the Zalud family is still in their home welcoming you as guests. So, be kind, and be good guests to your hosts.

4

LAS CRUCES ADOBE

Gaviota State Park just north of Santa Barbara is known for its beaches, state park and beautiful scenery. It is a much sought-after place for families to go camping, is a stopping point for travelers on their way to points farther north and serves as the turnoff for those heading into Lompoc and La Purisima Mission. Its nearness to the tourist town of Solvang with its old-world Danish charm means that thousands of folks pass thorough, many without knowing that history is just outside their car windows. This is because Gaviota is also home to the Las Cruces Adobe. This adobe was once a stage and rest stop and a small town with a few stores and amusements but is now only a shell of what once was. Las Cruces today is nothing more than a ghost town with one building remaining, overseen by the state parks department, and is now said to be one of the most haunted spots in Santa Barbara County.

It is said that in the early 1800s, a vicious battle took place between the Native Chumash People and Spanish soldiers. The Chumash had a large village at the site of Gaviota Creek, and their village was in the way of the Spanish El Camino Real trail being developed for the creation of the new mission system. This created tension between the two peoples, and a battle took place in which many Chumash were killed. After the fight, the Chumash graves were marked by the Native survivors with totems, seashells and other symbols of their faith. Later on, Franciscan priests replaced these headstones with Christian crosses. After the new Christian markers were placed on more than one hundred graves, the area became known as "The

The road to the Las Cruces Adobe is shaded and dark, giving one a taste of what they can expect from the adobe itself.

Crosses," or *Las Cruces* in Spanish. It wasn't long before a town sprang up, and travelers began to notice the area as a place they could stop before continuing on to Northern California.

By 1864, a stagecoach route through the Gaviota Pass had been planned, and Las Cruces vied for a stage stop to be placed in their town. The citizens knew it would be the perfect spot to rest, water horses and provision people before heading up the mountains to Santa Ynez or Lompoc. Having a stage stop in their town would mean more income for Las Cruces by providing food and lodging to the folks traveling on the stage, as well as the stage operators paying for the care of their horses. Knowing how lucrative the stop could be, competition between the townsfolk became savage for who would get the contract, and it would eventually end in murder.

The stop was finally put in place, and it did bring prosperity to the small town; however, it wasn't until 1875 that traffic through town drastically increased. That is the year that the Hollister and Dibblee families constructed a wharf at Gaviota for the purpose of exporting their supplies of wool. Not only was the wharf used by these two families, but it also became the major exporting site for the farmers of the Santa Ynez and Lompoc valleys to get their goods to market. Farmers, many of whom came from miles away, would drop off their farm exports at the wharf and then stay the night in Las Cruces before making their way back home the following morning.

By 1877, Las Cruces had grown to include a hotel, store and post office, all housed in the stagecoach stop. It was during this period that the stagecoach stop also became a notorious brothel and whiskey emporium. When whiskey, prostitutes and young men who fancy themselves gunfighters combine, it rarely ends well, and records show that gunfights, robberies and other mayhem occurred during this time in the town's history. Even with the lawless element in town, Las Cruces thrived, and things looked good for the little town.

As the automobile burst onto the scene and America began its inevitable car culture, Las Cruces adapted with the times, and an inn, store, gas station and other businesses catering to the passing motorists were built. Even still, the population of the town began to dwindle as folks headed for larger towns and cities where life moved faster. As the Pacific Coast Highway was rerouted to connect with the new US 101 Highway, traffic all but stopped coming to Las Cruces. There were the occasional tourists who passed through but only because they had heard about the quaint little town; they rarely stopped. The town became nothing more than a passing

The adobe building is all that remains of the town of Las Cruces.

interest to be driven through out of curiosity on the way to somewhere else. Progress was killing Las Cruces.

As the cars and travelers slowed, more and more folks left town until Las Cruces was finally completely abandoned. Over the years since citizens began leaving, the structures were either demolished or decayed as Mother Nature reclaimed the land. When the California State Parks Department purchased the surrounding area from the Hollister family in 1967, to become part of Gaviota State Park, the only building still standing was the adobe that had been the stage stop. Today, there is nothing left to show a small town ever stood in this area of California, save for the now fenced-off Las Cruces Adobe. Gone are any remnants of what was one of the most historic sites in northern Santa Barbara County. Luckily, the State Parks Department keeps this last symbol of the once growing town secure behind a fence and underneath a protective roof. It has classified, and rightly so, the Las Cruces Adobe as a historic site and one to be preserved for future generations.

The town of Las Cruces may be gone, its structures returned to the earth and the site nothing more than a memory for the few who take notice. It is uncommon today to see folks visiting this small-town site on the outskirts of Gaviota and Lompoc. But for those who venture out to Las Cruces, it becomes clear the town really isn't abandoned. There are still residents who reside here, still call the town home and will never leave it. For you see, Las Cruces is now a place the dead call home.

As mentioned earlier, the combination of gambling, whiskey and illicit sex is one that can very easily turn what would normally be a pleasant atmosphere into one of violence and murder. This lawless element that existed for a brief time in the town of Las Cruces left an indelible mark on the land. It wasn't just the lawlessness itself but the fact that the Spanish, even in an attempt at honoring the Chumash who had been killed, unintentionally desecrated the graves of Native Americans. This desecration also violated the families who had left offerings on the graves and the very customs that governed the treatment of the Chumash People. These types of events often keep the dead from moving on to their afterlife. This seems to be what is happening at this historic adobe.

When the Spanish padres removed the various offerings the Chumash People had left for their honored dead, it was meant as a show of respect for the people killed by the Spanish soldiers. However, as all of the Christian crosses that replaced the original markers were made of wood, over the years the crosses began to decay and turn to dust. Once the Spanish ceded California to Mexico, the new government had neither the means nor the interest in keeping this small grave site in order. Once the United States took

Only cactus marks the graves that once honored the Chumash People at Las Cruces.

control, most, if not all of the crosses were gone, and the few that remained were removed to make way for the stage stop. Today, over one hundred Native American graves remain lost, lying unmarked somewhere near the town of Las Cruces.

Folks who have come to visit the area while staying at Gaviota State Park have reported seeing the shadows of these Chumash warriors. They are often seen standing in the distance, staring at those visiting the site. They are rarely seen for any length of time and will simply vanish from sight. Some who have tried to approach these specters claim that as they draw near the warrior will simply shake his head, turn and disappear. No one is sure if these spirits are those of the Natives buried in the lost cemetery or the ghosts of their people who have come to keep an eye on their lost brothers. These Chumash are not relegated to the area around the adobe but have been seen in the campgrounds and on the beaches of Gaviota. As this entire area was Chumash land, it is not hard to understand their protectiveness for what they still claim as theirs.

Very little remains of the adobe, and what little is left is surrounded by a chain-link fence to keep scavengers from taking the rest as souvenirs. The adobe was the actual stage stop, and it was here that the saloon, and brothel were established. It is said that quite a few gunfights broke out at the saloon, with drunk gamblers either claiming to have been cheated or having been caught. How many gunslingers, gamblers and drunks were killed in and around the adobe has been lost to time, but there is at least one who has never left the place where he was killed. Many folks who tour the site have said they have seen an apparition wearing clothing "right out of a western movie," complete with a long black trench coat, black hat and gun belt. Whether or not he was involved in a gunfight inside or outside of the adobe, it seems clear that he lost the fight. On rare occasions, he has been seen reliving his death, but the scene stops just before any shots have, or would have, been fired.

There is a legend that has grown over the years about three prostitutes who were murdered at the adobe when it was functioning as a brothel. It is said that two of these soiled doves were strangled by an irate customer. The story says that the john was upset about the cost of the girls, didn't want to pay and killed the ladies. The third lady of the evening is said to have died by suicide; why she took her life is not known or not told. These soiled doves are often seen walking about inside the old adobe. Reports that have come from those who have seen them say it looks as if they are still going about plying their trade. Folks claim the apparitions will flit about the room as

Be careful peering onto the dark recesses of the Las Cruces Adobe; you just may see something looking back.

if talking to people, then walk toward where the rooms used to be before disappearing. Many believe that these spirits are unaware they have passed through the veil, and to them they are in the time before their passing. It is hoped that one day these lost ladies will find peace and a renewed purpose in the afterlife.

With so much history in and around Gaviota State Park, it is a perfect place for the ParaTraveler to use as a base for exploring the many haunts in the area; La Purisima, Santa Maria, Ventura and of course Las Cruces Adobe are just a short drive away. Buellton, where Anderson's Pea Soup Restaurant was once located, which is said to be haunted, is on the way to Solvang, and both should be visited while in the neighborhood to complete any visit to the Santa Barbara area. Just remember when visiting these locations, even if you think you are alone, you may have companions you can't see but who can see you. Be kind, say hello and wish them a happy eternity.

5
SILVER CITY GHOST TOWN

There are many people who love what has come to be called "ghost towning." They visit ghost towns all around the state, snapping pictures, learning the sites' history and discovering how they became empty and all but forgotten. These towns were once thriving mining communities, logging towns and transport hubs, and all fell victim to a decline in the ore and minerals that had kept them alive. Ghost towns have become tourist attractions. But what happens when a town becomes defunct, is scheduled for demolition and is to be erased from the land? You build Silver City Ghost Town, of course.

Silver City in Bodfish, California, is not a true ghost town. It is, however, a historical museum devoted to the preservation of the history of the Kern River valley and the many towns that once thrived among the mountains of the Sierra. Dave and Arvilla Mills came up with the idea of starting their own Knott's Berry Farm–style amusement park in 1968 and began collecting buildings that were about to be torn down at many of the towns around the Kern River valley. So, by 1972, the Millses had saved structures from nearby Keysville, Claraville, old-town Isabella, Whisky Flats, Miracle, South Fork and many others. The amusement park never came to pass, but Dave and Arvilla's dedication to saving the history of the area was such that they created Silver City Ghost Town as a way to showcase the towns that had been lost in the name of progress.

Silver City Ghost Town opened in 1968 and was a huge success. As it was situated on the main road coming from Bakersfield, those traveling to Lake

It is hard to believe that Silver City is nothing more than a collection of historic buildings and not an actual ghost town.

Isabella, the tourist town of Kernville or up to the Trail of 100 Giants Sequoia tree grove had to drive past Silver City on the way to their destination. Many would stop in on their way up or on the return trip to marvel at the structures now arranged to resemble an actual town from the valley, ask questions of the Millses regarding the history of the town and buildings, then leave with a greater knowledge of the area than when they arrived. Their dream seemed to have come true. Then, the alignment of California Highway 178 was changed and so were the fortunes of Silver City.

To make it easier for travelers to get to the beautiful lake, the Kern River, the natural wonders of the valley and beyond, old Highway 178 was rerouted, straightened and consequently thoroughly bypassed Bodfish and Silver City. Where once thousands of cars passed the museum town, now only a handful passed by each day, and those were mostly local traffic. Even with signs on the new roadway advertising the town, people just stopped coming. Three years after Silver City opened, the Millses shut it down and built a tall fence around it. Silver City sat empty and all but forgotten. Most of the locals figured the town had been torn down, and others, if it crossed their minds at all, just assumed it had worn away and collapsed from the elements. This was not the case, however, and everyone found out that the town was still there and viable when, in 1988, J Paul Corlew purchased Silver City and the surrounding properties with the idea of bringing the old museum back to life. And bring it back he did.

For the next four years, Corlew refurbished the now dilapidated town, carefully restored the buildings to historical accuracy and built a gift shop and antique store out front. Folks could now browse all sorts of interesting artifacts, and buy both secondhand items and treasures found among the ruins of the now defunct towns of the valley. Once again, folks could learn the history of this mostly forgotten area of California. Corlew reopened Silver City Ghost Town on Memorial Day weekend in 1992 and has kept it alive to this day. Each building in the ghost town has its own unique history and story, some of which are a marvel in the telling. From a gunslinger who may have been the fastest draw to ever live, the house once owned by the founding family of the valley and a jail that should be under water but instead still lives out in the air and sunshine, each has its own resident spirit. Most of the structures at Silver City are known to be haunted, and guests have sent many photographs that are on display in the gift shop for those interested. J Paul Corlew passed away in late 2021, and his son Shawn now runs the town. Shawn has said that he will try to keep the town as his father wanted. With its reputation for being haunted, it wouldn't be a surprise to find that J is still around making sure the town he loved is looked after.

Over the years since J Paul Corlew reopened Silver City, the town has been featured in many television news segments and paranormal shows. The hauntings began well before Corlew bought the town, but after its reopening, the activity seemed to grow and has not diminished to this day. One of the more pronounced events to have occurred here took place in the Apalatea/ Burlando House. This structure is perhaps the oldest in the Kern area, and it was originally the home for the founders of the valley, the Apalatea family. One Halloween night while Corlew was hosting one of the town's Lantern Light ghost tours, he heard a commotion coming from the Apalatea House, where some guests had gathered to see if any spirits were present. By the time Corlew arrived at the house, things had calmed down, but his guests began telling him that massive poltergeist activity had just taken place. Corlew had repurposed the interior of the home to look like a saloon from the Wild West days of the valley. Folks told him that glasses had been floating from one area of the bar to another; whiskey bottles had flown off shelves, spun around the room and then crashed down to the floor or one of the tables set around the room. Others told him that a few of the mannequins he had placed at the tables actually turned their heads to look at the guests before turning back

The bottles in the Berlando House will move on their own, and the mannequins have been known to turn their heads and look at guests who stare in their direction.

to the poker hands in front of them or to the faux drinks set on the tables. A few even complimented him for having "great special effects" set up for his guests. After word got out about this amazing event, the TV show *This Old House* came out and the crew did its own investigation, which prompted host Bob Vila to pronounce Silver City Ghost Town as the number 1 spot in the country for poltergeist activity.

As mentioned above, the old Whisky Flat jail should be under Lake Isabella but was saved by the Millses. Whisky Flat became a victim of the dam project when the Kern River was backed up to create the lake. During the time the jail was in operation, it "hosted" quite a few unsavory characters. One of these colorful scoundrels was Newt Walker. Walker was a gunslinger, businessman and gambler; he was also said to be the fasted draw to ever live. In 1905, Newton "Newt" Walker killed two men in self-defense but was charged with murder for the killings. Walker outdrew the two men even though Walker's back had been turned, and the unlikelihood of a man outdrawing two other men with a head start was such that the judge needed proof of the act. Walker provided that proof, and he was acquitted. Newt, having spent time in the Whisky Flat jail now residing at Silver City, is said to make an appearance at the lockup from time to time to this day.

Another spirit said to haunt the old jail and make itself known often is that of a Native American who, trying to stay warm on a cold winter night, lit a fire by the jail door and burned to death as a result. Over the years, many people entering the jail report seeing the figure of a man sleeping in the front corner of the structure. At first, thinking the man is an employee, many will try to stay as quiet as possible so as not to wake him and are shocked when the figure slowly fades from view before their eyes. This spirit is seen in the exact spot where the doomed man was found the morning after his horrendous death.

The old Hot Springs Baptist Church is another building where a lot of paranormal activity has taken place. One of the more pronounced occurrences happened when former *Ghost Hunters* star Brandon Alvis was alone in the church one night. While conducting an audio session in the church, Alvis was asking questions when unexpectedly his cameras went wonky. At the same time, a menacing voice demanded in no uncertain terms he "get out." This author has had similar things happen while investigating the church, as have others. It would seem that whoever has taken up residency in the old church wants to be left alone. Many times during the museum's Lantern Light Tours, guests have been touched, pushed and heard voices asking them to leave.

Perhaps the most haunted building at Silver City is that of Anne "Wormie Annie" Sullivan's bait shop. This is one of the only buildings original to the property, and it would seem that Annie doesn't mind folks visiting her old bait shop but actually enjoys it. Annie has been seen in the shop so many times that it can no longer be doubted that she is still there looking after her shop or the town. Pictures of Annie, who had recognizable features, have been snapped almost daily, and those who have sensed her presence during Lantern Light Tours have felt her warm and friendly personality.

Having guest hosted some of these tours for years I have seen Annie on more than one occasion and been witness to what I have dubbed the "vortex mirror." When you stare into the mirror in the back of the bait shop, faces other than your own begin to surface. I have seen this more than once, with the faces and their positions in the mirror glass changing with each viewing. To this day, no one knows why this happens or who the specters may be. What we do know is Annie always welcomes folks to her shop with open arms, and no one has ever felt threatened in her bait shop.

The entire town is teeming with spirits, and so many folks have witnessed this that the town's reputation is now that of a haunted ghost town. I have seen so many things here over the years that I cannot deny the reputation is

With the amount of spirit activity at Silver City, it isn't hard to imagine a ghost hanging from the tree.

well deserved. From the ghostly cowboy seen strolling down the boardwalks, the spirits still residing in the old bunkhouse, the shadow spirits seen lurking in the dark recesses and the faces that peer out into the town from the gift shop, Silver City is one of the most haunted places one can visit. The owner even allows private investigations for those with the fortitude to give it a go.

Over the years, J Paul Corlew and his son became family. I am happy Shawn has decided to carry on his father's work and dedication to the history and haunts of the Kern River valley and always look forward to seeing them both; for you see, I believe that my friend J is still there entertaining and educating his guests.

6

LONE PINE

L one Pine, California, sits just to the north of the now mostly dried up Owens Lake in the Owens Valley. Set between the Panamint Mountains on the east and the Sierra on the west, this little town is big in history. Mount Whitney is the tallest peak in the contiguous United States, and the road that leads to the trailhead is reached by driving into Lone Pine. The lowest point in the contiguous United States is in Death Valley, and a road leading there is picked up on the southern border of the town. From Lone Pine, one can drive to the highest spot in the country, then the lowest, and still make it back in time to have a nice dinner and a stay in one of the town's haunted hotels. The day after your drive, it will be time to visit the many haunted hot spots Lone Pine has to offer.

Lone Pine has had a long past, and history breeds legends, lore and spirits. This town is no exception, as one can find spirits all over the area. One such haunted section is the aforementioned Whitney Portal Road. It is said that the sounds of a long past battle that took place between the U.S. Army and Native Paiute people can still be heard while driving along Whitney Portal Road. This road, the only one with a traffic light that crosses Highway 395 in the small town, passes right through the battleground. The battle was fierce and took place when Lone Pine was still a small supply stop. Over the many years since homes were built along Whitney Portal Road, people have reported hearing the sounds of gunfire, screams of agony and men clashing. It is said that one woman looked out of her window to see a Paiute warrior looking back at her. The warrior ignored

The town of Lone Pine lies at the northern edge of the now dry Owen's Lake.

her as he rushed off toward the sounds of the raging battle. Others who live near the site where the clash took place have even seen this spectral battle raging around them, and many who have not become used to the sights and sounds are afraid to leave their homes and have actually called the police to report a war raging in their neighborhood. Many people assume that ghostly activity comes only in the darkness of night, but the people in this area hear the sounds of warfare both day and night. There seems to be no rhyme or reason as to when the spirits begin their fight, but many locals have become accustomed to the sounds.

Another spirit often seen along Whitney Portal Road is that of Indian Jim. Jim was a prospector in the area around the 1940s. The Sierra Range is a harsh environment, and even those familiar with its idiosyncrasies can and will be surprised by the sudden turns of weather. This is what happened to Jim. Caught in an abrupt blizzard, Indian Jim froze to death before he could get to the safety of shelter. For those who knew the man before death, they say he was a kind person who never bothered anyone and mainly stayed to himself—this was in life, of course. Today, Jim still mainly stays to himself, unless he is needed. When Jim sees folks in trouble, he will step in and try to aid them. He has saved many after his own death.

Jim has taken it upon himself to warn people roaming the Alabama Hills and surrounding area about incoming, severe storms. Jim will approach those who are in need of warning, but only close enough to be heard, and point in the direction of Lone Pine. Jim will then utter a single word, "Go." Jim has saved many people just before deadly rain or snowstorms have hit the area. It is believed by some that Jim has become a self-appointed ranger to try to make sure others do not suffer the same fate. Others think that Jim must remain to atone for past wrongs and will only pass on when his penance has been paid. Whatever one believes, Indian Jim has garnered the new nickname of Rescue Man. If you ever see this kindly soul, you'd best heed his warning and make a run for Lone Pine and safety.

Owens Lake was not always a dry, alkali salt flat. Before the City of Los Angeles stole and continues to steal the precious water the valley needs, Owens Lake was the largest lake in California. As such, the entire area was highly sought after by both the Native Paiute people and the U.S. Cavalry. As usually seems to happen in these cases, war would usually break out with one side trying to kill the other. This was the case during the Owens Valley–Paiute War, and one of the biggest battles of the conflict took place right along the shores of Owens Lake.

There have been numerous reports, albeit not for many years, of a ghostly battle taking place between Owens Valley Paiute and the U.S. Army along the shores of the Owens Lake. Witnesses say that both warriors and soldiers can be seen falling from their horses, being trampled by their own steeds and fighting so fierce that the combatants' blood can be smelled by those looking on. It is said that the men and horses looked as real and solid as everything else around them. The tales that are told, along with the description of what was seen, coincided exactly with the battle that took place there many years earlier.

The Dow Villa Hotel in the heart of Lone Pine is said to be haunted by those Hollywood celebrities for whom it was built and others who have stayed while driving Highway 395 on their way to Carson City. This historic hotel/motel was built in the 1920s for Hollywood actors, and over the years it has seen stars such as John Wayne, Clint Eastwood, Roy Rogers, Ida Lupino and Anne Baxter; even Captain Kirk, William Shatner, stayed at the Dow Villa Hotel. These actors and actresses have been coming to Lone Pine to film in the Alabama Hills, one of the main backdrops for western shoot-em-ups and alien worlds, since the early days of film, and it would seem that some past guests decided to remain. Over the years, spirits have been seen walking the corridors of the old hotel. Folks staying here have been awakened in the middle of the night by someone sitting on the edge of their beds or, on occasion, getting into bed with them. Since many of the rooms in the hotel have a shared bathroom, it is not uncommon for the door to be shut and locked when someone comes to use the loo. There have been times, as guests wait, when the door will suddenly open as if the one using the room is finished, yet no one will ever emerge from the bathroom. When the room is entered, it will be completely empty. These reports come only from the hotel. The motel section, which was built much later than the hotel, has never had a single report of activity.

The other haunted hotel in Lone Pine is one that you would not expect to be haunted. The Best Western Frontier Hotel is just inside town as you enter from the south. This modern, up-to-date hotel is said to be haunted by a cowboy that is often seen walking down the outside walkways, usually in the early morning or at dusk. He is sometimes seen in the rooms as a guest enters but will quickly leave with a tip of his hat and a brief smile. No one knows who this gentleman cowboy is, yet he has always been courteous.

There is one other odd tale regarding the town, and it is not about a spirit but rather a strange creature that lurks in the hills. Some have said that the Lone Pine Mountain Devil is the West Coast cousin of the New Jersey Devil. The Lone Pine Mountain Devil has supposedly been around since the days when the Spanish began colonizing California and was first reported by a Spanish padre who walked out of the wilderness after his wagon train was attacked by the beast. When Father Justus Martinez arrived at the San Gabriel Mission and told his story to the priests on his arrival, they couldn't believe what they were hearing. They first thought that all of those he traveled with had been killed by Lucifer in the form of a lizard-like creature with wings. The monster had eaten the settlers—but only their torsos—and devoured all thirty-six humans in one meal. Martinez said that the only reason he survived was because he had camped away from the group, not wanting to get involved with their debauchery, while the creature went about its evil work. The padre believed that the creature acted in retribution for the burning of the forest trees used in the campfires.

There have been no sightings of the Lone Pine Mountain Devil since 1928, and some folks reasoned that it was due to the influx of people moving to the area as well as tourists passing through or the fact that the water was stolen from the Owens Valley. Whatever the reason, the reports all but stopped until the early 2000s.

With the rise of the internet, sightings of this creature again began to pour in. Reports of people mysteriously disappearing from the Alabama Hills, Death Valley and Whitney Portal as well as the peak itself became common. Many believe that the Lone Pine Mountain Devil is nothing more

The Alabama Hills on the outskirts of Lone Pine, with their otherworldly landscapes, have been used in many sci-fi and western films. It is also a great place to camp.

than an internet hoax. I, for one, would not bet my life on it and remain vigilant, just in case, every time I camp in the area.

Lone Pine is one of those towns a lot of people have never heard of, but once they do and visit this place nestled between two beautiful mountain ranges, they usually come back for another visit or five. For those of you on the hunt for spirits, Lone Pine is just what you are looking for: it has movie history, beautiful scenery that can compete with any alpine vista and a plethora of ghosts to make even the skeptical ParaTraveler a believer.

7

CALICO GHOST TOWN

Most people don't look at the Mojave Desert and think about ghosts. But if one knows the history of this desert, a place that has the hottest location on earth in its midst, along with legends of lost wagon trains and thirst, they wouldn't be surprised to find one of the most haunted places in the country here. I am talking about the official Silver Rush Ghost Town of California and a place that spawned one of the best amusement parks in the state or perhaps the country, Calico Ghost Town. You may be thinking, how could such a small town have so many haunted places within its boundaries? I thought the same thing before starting research on my book *Ghosts and Legends of Calico*. It would seem that all the buildings, and most of the large mines here, have at least one ghost that calls the place home.

Calico was a thriving silver mining town from about 1882 until the end of the 1800s. The town began to decline at the turn of the century and was finally abandoned, save for Lucy Lane, just as the 1940s began. The town decayed and was almost lost when Walter Knott—co-creator of the boysenberry, onetime resident and employee of Calico and the man who used Calico as the inspiration for his amusement park ghost town, Knott's Berry Farm—stepped in and saved the most profitable silver mine in California for future generations.

While writing my book about Calico, the number of tales I was receiving from current employees was astounding. Food is one of those things that is a must in a tourist museum town, and it seems the spirits at Calico like to hang out where the food is. Lil's Saloon was once Dr. Rhea's office and pharmacy.

Almost every single building at Calico Ghost Town has a resident spirit.

Not having much need for either in a tourist stop, the building near the center of town was repurposed to serve pizza, hot dogs and beer. The actors, who portray both good guys and bad guys in mock shoot-outs, would come to relax in Lil's once the day was through, and it has become a tradition since. There are times, however, when the employees of Lil's will be working in the back cleaning, closing up after all have left, and they hear the sound of people in the dining room. They will go out to investigate the noise, figuring that some cast members, not realizing the saloon is closed, are waiting for service. The talking will continue right up until they enter the dining room. As soon as they enter, all noise stops, and the room is completely empty. Other times, guests sitting at the tables will feel like someone has brushed past them even when no one has passed by or is near them.

The Old Miner's Café, sitting up on a hill near the schoolhouse, is haunted by spirits that argue and another that likes to move things around in the stockroom. On other occasions, the spirit tosses buns at the cook. Even the two popcorn carts in town have spirits attached to them, but perhaps the most interesting dining experience comes from the only full-service restaurant in town, the Calico House Restaurant. Here you will find a spirit who likes to turn up the radio so loud that one cannot hear themselves think and likes to call out people's names at random times. The most disturbing thing that happens at the Calico House comes about when the restaurant is closed. A mysterious shadow figure has been seen crossing the street in front of the eatery and passing into the lot on the opposite side. This usually happens after dark, and many taking the nightly ghost walk have seen this strange apparition. The Sweet Shop and Dorsey's Dog House, which caters to our four-legged friends, also have resident ghosts.

The mines in and around Calico have been known as hot spots for paranormal activity. One, the Maggie Mine, directly in the center of town, has had reports of not only ghosts but also tommyknocker activity. Tommyknockers are fairy creatures who inhabit and work the mines next to their human kin. These beings, depending on how they are treated by humans, will either be menacing or kind, albeit with a mischievous streak toward their human counterparts. As far as ghosts are concerned, reports of hearing the sounds of miners still toiling away in the now closed mine are frequent. Guests touring the Maggie Mine have seen apparitions within the mine and what many call "zombie-looking" spirits descending the stairway that leads to the exit of the mine. Many a guest has decided to go back the way they had come rather than hazard the stairs where these specters have been seen. The Maggie Mine is not to be missed for those looking for possible paranormal activity.

The Calico School House has become famous for a spectral schoolmarm who likes to educate guests of the town.

As mentioned, almost every single building in Calico appears to be haunted. That includes the shops and amusements that line both sides of the town's street. One of the places that seems to have the most activity would be R&D Fossils and Minerals. This store sells everything from gems, stones and magnets to clothes. It also seems to be the favorite haunt of the town's founder, Sheriff John King. King has been seen walking in the store, following shoppers, and seems to hate Elvis Presley music. Every time Elvis is played, the radio will suddenly turn off or the dial will be switched to country music. King has also become protective of those who work at the store. He will sometimes be seen sitting in the office chair, watching the store as if keeping an eye on things. Other shops where spirits have been seen or heard include the candle shop, woodworking store and Calico Print Shop. The print shop sells books and other tourist fare and seems to have a cowboy that can be a bit mischievous but also seems to like kids.

Lucy Lane, who lived in Calico from 1882 until her death in 1967, is often seen walking across the street from Lane's General Store, the same store she and her husband once owned, to her house, which is directly across the street. Lane's house is now a museum dedicated to the Granddame of Calico and the town itself. Lucy is known to keep watch over her house, as is her husband, John, who has made himself known at both locations.

The Calico Cemetery has so many lost graves that no one is sure how many folks are buried here.

From "Tumbleweed" Harris, longtime beloved street performer and Calico town "sheriff," to Dorsey the Dog walking along the streets and lying on the porch at the Calico Print Shop, there is little doubt that Calico has its fair share of ghosts still calling the town home. And from the cemetery with its lost graves to the mines that echo the voices of those lost to accidents, the spirits of Calico call out. Even from the town office, where the rangers say ghosts don't exist, I have heard tales from others in the town about soiled doves who once called these offices home appearing to visitors. The rangers at the town once told me that "Calico is a famous ghost town, not a famous town of ghosts." It seems to me that those working here, as well as the ghosts themselves, would dispute the rangers' claims.

8

THE AMARGOSA HOTEL
AND OPERA HOUSE

Death Valley, California, is not simply a name on a map or a place where a cute nickname grew out of the dust of the Mojave Desert. No, Death Valley truly is as the name implies. A place of death. Death Valley is not only the lowest place in the United States of America but also the hottest place on earth. Here, temperatures routinely hit 120 degrees Fahrenheit, and the highest on the planet was recorded here on July 10, 1913, at 134 degrees at Furnace Creek. The entire area receives only approximately two inches of rain each year, and often, thunderstorms will produce deadly flooding. During the 1800s migration west, wagon trains trying to reach the Pacific found water scarce, and many died from thirst. Others simply went mad from the heat and wandered off into the terminal sunshine, never to be seen again. With conditions such as these, it is a wonder that anyone would choose to live here, but that is exactly what they did. Drawn by dreams of riches from gold, silver and other precious metals, folks came, toiled, lived and died in one of the deadliest places one could imagine: Death Valley, California.

Folks had been coming here to search for wealth since gold and silver were discovered nearby. When borax was found, with the many uses it could provide, it became a top commodity in the barren landscape of the Mojave Desert. The town of Amargosa was begun in 1907, when the Tonopah and Tidewater Railroad was constructed, and a spur line with loading site for the Lila C. Mine was needed. The Pacific Borax Company decided that the area, just twenty-seven miles from Furnace Creek, would be the best spot for

Above: The Amargosa Hotel is struggling to survive in the harsh Death Valley sun.

Left: The Amargosa Opera House was the brainchild of Marta Becket, and because of her dedication, the old opera house is now on the National Register of Historic Places.

such a rail stop. It wasn't long before the company had the idea of building a center where employees could come to relax and a place where investors could come and enjoy all that the Mojave Desert had to offer.

When first opened, the complex was a U-shaped Spanish Revival building replete with company offices, a plush lobby, a store, a dormitory that could accommodate twenty-three company miners and a social room. At one end of this complex, a large hall was designed for community gatherings, from church services to dancing, and later used as a movie theater. Over time, Death Valley Junction began to grow. The company building already housed a café, and a restaurant was added to the town, along with a large gas station and a repair garage for both automobiles that were beginning to come through as well as the trucks used for hauling borax coming from the mines. It looked as though Death Valley Junction was here to stay. That is, until the railroad stopped running.

By 1942, the Tonopah and Tidewater Railroad was no longer a profitable endeavor. In 1942, the railroad was shut down, the rails went to Egypt for the war effort and the Pacific Borax Company left Death Valley Junction. Over the next few years, the town began a slow decay back into the desert. People still remained in town, but as many moved on, the buildings left behind were reclaimed by the Mojave. The community center, hotel and surrounding land went through several owners, but none of them put much time or money into the upkeep of the center. By the late 1960s, the entire building had begun to fade away, as had most of the rest of Death Valley Junction.

In 1967, a dancer by the name of Marta Becket drove into town on her way west. Her car broke down, and as there was no one there to fix it, she made arrangements to have it picked up but would have to stay in Death Valley Junction for a day or two. While staying in town, Marta wandered over to Corkhill Hall, which was the name of the community center, peeked through the keyhole and saw what would become her dream. Having already fallen in love with the remote beauty of the town and the desert, finding a hall where she could build the dance theater of her dreams was more than she could imagine.

Over the next few years, Marta repaired the old community center, installed seats, painted the walls with murals to rival Doris Zinkeisen and renamed the community center, now known as the opera house Amargosa, after the town's original name (*amargosa* is Spanish for "bitter"). After opening the Amargosa Opera House and Hotel, Marta gave daily shows, mostly to an empty house, but whether her audience was one hundred or none, she would give it her all. Marta was a consummate professional who lived and breathed dance and entertainment. Marta would live, dance and perform in Amargosa for the rest of her life and continued to dance on the stage she built well into her eighties. Marta Becket passed away in January 2017, but the legacy she built with her own two hands still welcomes guests to Death Valley and the opera house to this day.

The Amargosa Opera House and Hotel was added to the National Register of Historic Places in 1981, and today it is run by a nonprofit group dedicated to keeping the history of Death Valley Junction alive for future generations. The hotel rooms feature cherubs, statutes, peacock feathers and murals, and the guest dining room is painted to represent a Spanish courtyard. The most historic room at the hotel, room 22, where longtime friend of Marta's, Red Skelton stayed on numerous occasions, is adorned with a mural of a ballerina dancing on a ball while balancing on a string surrounded by acrobats performing a special dedication to Marta's dear friend Red.

The history of the Amargosa Opera House and Hotel is long, and that of the town it rests in is longer. From miners and railroad workers to gamblers and travelers, today's Death Valley Junction has seen and done it all. So many folks have passed through that even in this out-of-the-way location, in the most inhospitable place on earth, the numbers are too great to count. Stranger still are those who lived and died here who have remained in this hell on earth (weather wise) long after death has claimed them.

Many folks who have come to visit the Amargosa Hotel have found more than they bargained for. Tales of the supernatural seem to have become commonplace here, and even though none of the hauntings are dangerous, for the uninitiated, they can be disturbing if encountered unawares. One of the most interesting spirits at the opera house is that of a spectral cat. No one is sure where the cat came from or whose cat it might have been, but it has been around the opera house for as long as anyone can remember. On more than one occasion, Marta would be deep into one of her dance routines when the cat would saunter across the stage and interrupt the dancer's rhythm. Marta, of course, would simply recompose herself and continue, even while being amused at the looks on the faces of her audience. Another figure who seemingly haunts the theater is Marta's onetime partner Tom Willet. Tom has been spotted sitting in various seats during Marta's presentations and always appears to be thoroughly enjoying the show. Many years ago, a guest who had been sitting next to Tom and commenting to him throughout the performance was flabbergasted to find the seat empty as the lights came up.

The "sleepy hollow" section of the hotel, now off-limits to guests, is said to be one of the most haunted areas of the property. *Courtesy of Joe Ruffulo.*

The hotel dining room has had its share of ghostly tales; people have claimed to hear disembodied voices carrying on as if a group of folks are having a gathering that isn't there. Folks have said that on more than one occasion, spontaneous sounds of a party will erupt, linger for a few moments and then be gone as quickly as they came. One spirit that always seems to stand out is that of a woman with an especially high-pitched voice.

There is an area of the hotel in the back of the building that has come to be known as "spooky hollow." This area was once the dormitory of the borax mine workers and was where the hospital and morgue were located. The area is now off-limits to guests, but tours are given, and it has become well known as the most haunted area of the property. Shadow people have become a common occurrence in this area, and even though the location is no longer accessible, folks who come near often hear the sounds of conversations and see apparitions walking about. It was in this area a few years back that a movie was being filmed, and during editing, the crew noticed a person in the frame who could not be accounted for and seemed quite transparent. This has happened on more than one occasion during both film and music video shoots over the years.

The hotel has been known to have a few resident spirits roaming about as well. Room 32 is perhaps the one with the darkest reputation and one you might want to avoid if you are not a consummate ParaTraveler. This room is said to be haunted by one of the old mining bosses. It is said that even in life the man was a cruel master and would routinely abuse those under him. It would seem that death has not tempered his mood or his manners. Guests who have stayed in this room have never reported physical abuse or manifestations, but many have had feelings come over them that can only be described as apprehension and severe anxiety. Many have had chills that cannot be warmed even with layers of blankets. It would seem that even in death, this mean taskmaster still wants his due.

Room 24 is another one of the rooms where quite a few reports of paranormal activity have come to light. Here, folks have heard the sound of a child crying during the night. Many folks have gone looking for the child, thinking a kid has possibly gotten locked out of their room by mistake, but no matter how hard they look, no child can be found, yet the crying remains. In the morning, these guests will be told that no child was staying at the hotel, adding to the lodger's confusion. There is an urban legend of a young girl who had drowned in the bathtub of the room in 1967; could this be the truth behind the tale?

Room 9 is said to be the most haunted room at the Amargosa Hotel. Many folks have reported being awakened by the feeling of their legs being held down and finding that no matter how hard they try, they cannot move their legs or feet. It lasts only a few moments, but that feeling can be overwhelming. At other times, guests will see and hear the doorknob turn followed by a slight knock, but when they go to open the door, there is no one there. As they start to close the door, they will hear the sounds of small feet running down the hallway and catch the amused sound of a little girl giggling as she runs away. Could this be the same child that is sometimes heard down the hall in room 24?

Other odd things that happen in and around the hotel are strange noises coming from the walls, footsteps that seem to cross the guest rooms at all hours of the day and night. Some have witnessed the sound of people walking down hallways, even though no one can be seen, and the scent of flowers where no flowers exist. Reports for every room at the hotel have come in about showers that will mysteriously turn on by themselves and then just as mysteriously turn off, and luggage looks as if it has been gone through while the guests are out of the room, even though the room was securely locked.

A few of the rooms at the Amargosa Hotel are said to have former guests who still enjoy the inn's accommodations.

No one who knows the Amargosa doubts that the location is haunted. Even the hotel used to run ghost hunts and paranormal tours before a novice and unscrupulous paranormal team ruined it for the rest of us. Many folks wonder if Marta herself has returned or never left the theater she built and loved. Considering how much Marta Becket cared for the entire area, I for one am sure she is still there looking after the location and enjoying her stage and cat.

9

THE MAJESTIC/VENTURA THEATER

The old Ventura Theater, now known as the Majestic, was built in the mid-1920s and opened its doors on August 16, 1928, to a full house. The event began with an organ solo by Paul Cowan, a few Paramount News clips and an episode of *Our Gang*; the feature film *Excess Baggage* followed, and the performance ended with a vaudeville show featuring the Ted Morse Recording Band with Evian & Armand, otherwise known as the Dancers Supreme. Folks had come to see not only the performance but also another amazing creation by the builders, who were already known for creating exceptional theaters. Hollywood developers Saul Lesser and Mike Rosenberg of Principal Theaters were well known for building elaborate movie theaters. So, when the two approached local Ventura theater owner C.C. Cocoran about a joint venture in building a brand-new, state-of-the-art theater for the community, he jumped at the chance. Architect Lewis Arthur Smith was hired to design the new theater; he had already created three well-known playhouses in Los Angeles: the Wilshire Theater, Beverly Theatre and Bard's Hollywood Theater. What Smith designed in Ventura was another Spanish Revival masterpiece that still stands in triumph to this day.

Smith created what has become known, as Jack Warner said, as "a movie palace." Ornate designs throughout the structure and decorations that rivaled European throne rooms and palaces were built. One of the most striking features was a model of a seventeenth-century Spanish brigantine ship lined with antique furniture, chairs and sofas so theatergoers could relax in the theater lobby. The interior of the huge theater auditorium had

The Ventura/Majestic is one of the oldest theaters in Ventura and likely the most haunted.

stenciled ceiling beams, a massive lighting system and a deep sky-blue ceiling behind a one-of-a-kind sunburst decoration, wall sconces and a double stairway with wrought-iron handrails that led up to an intimate balcony. It was, in every sense of the word, a movie *palace*.

All that remains of this grand interior today is perhaps the most expensive and distinctive decoration that adorned the Ventura Theater. That piece is the forty-foot "sun" concealing the main ceiling ventilator, and suspended from it hangs the handmade sunburst chandelier, which over the years, became as famous as the theater itself. Even though these pieces, along with the building design and permanent features are all that remain from the glory days of the Ventura Theater, there are other, less noticeable relics of the past that still adorn what has become the Majestic Theater of Ventura. You see, it is said that the Majestic still has some of its patrons, and perhaps an employee or two, who have decided that the old theater would be a good place to spend their afterlives. It would seem they aren't shy about letting the living know they are still there keeping an eye on them and the theater they have come to call home.

Most theaters have a haunted reputation, and the Ventura/Majestic is no exception; as a matter of fact, it may be one of the more haunted venues in

California. Today, the Majestic Theater is known as a concert venue and for its outstanding musical performances, but it is also known for its many spirits that give it character above its musical prowess. One of these spirits has become known as the theater's "what" ghost. The reason for this nickname is simple. This ghost will walk up behind folks, lean in close to their ears and simply say, "what"—nothing more, nothing less. No one knows who this spirit might be or why he is always asking people what, but some surmise that when folks enter an area that the ghost already occupies, he gets, shall we say, perturbed and wants to know why they are in his space. This spirit is found not only in one area of the Majestic but will ask his question all over the building, from the lobby and balcony to the backstage and equipment room. The "what" ghost, while frightening to some, has never been more than questioning, and employees of the theater have come to know him well enough that they simply apologize to him and move out of his space.

There is another spirit that resides at the Majestic that has come to be known as "Eddie." Eddie has been described as a "very nice spirit" by those who work at the Majestic; however, they go on to say that Eddie can be a bit protective of the theater. It is not uncommon for Eddie to push chairs in front of folks, almost, and even sometimes tripping them, if the spirit perceives that the individual has disrespected the venue or those who work there. It is not unheard of for Eddie to push folks or even trip them if he believes that their disrespect has reached an unacceptable level. It would seem that Eddie feels they should leave the theater and is letting them know he wants them to remove themselves from the premises. Eddie will oftentimes make himself known by coming up behind folks, looking over their shoulders and making sure they are behaving. He cannot be seen while doing this, but many guests to the theater have commented on feeling as if someone is watching them closely. For those Eddie feels have been OK but need reminding that this is his venue, he will move things around near them, just to let folks know he is there, and for others, he will "lose" things as a sterner example for the guests.

Even though the employees of the theater have mostly become used to the spirits at the Majestic, many try to make sure they are not the last to leave when closing up for the night. Some have said that when the lights go out, they can see things "floating" in their peripheral vision, and on occasion, it feels as if the darkness wants to "swallow you up." Nothing bad has ever happened to them working here, it's just a strange feeling that comes over them every once in a while. Another odd thing that has been reported here is the sound of footsteps coming down the aisles, followed by the sound of a "squeaky" seat being put down as if someone is about to sit in the theater chair. This happens in an otherwise empty house. It is as if a spectral audience has come to watch a show. This could be a residual haunting from the days when the Ventura Theater was still primarily a movie house. Another one of the ghosts in the balcony is that of an indistinct woman who is always seen as a blurry shadow and silhouetted by the light of a doorway as she walks past. No one is sure who she is, as the figure is always seen from a distance, so keep your eye out for her as you glance into the balcony from the seats below.

The backstage area is not off-limits to the spirits of the Majestic. Those operating the lighting and soundboard in the area below the stage have said that on many occasions, they will find the mixing boards have had their sliders moved after they have been set for the upcoming show. As the technician is resetting the sliders, they will be poked and nudged in a playful manner as if the spirits are having some fun with a friend. The boards are never messed with during a show, so this goes along with the playfulness, rather than any malicious intent by the ghost or ghosts. There are other times during practices and set up when the lights, sometimes those in the entire theater, will simply go off for no discernable reason. No matter how hard the employees try, they cannot get the lights to come back on. Then, as mysteriously as they went out, the lights will come on again. Like the mixing boards, this never happens during a show or when guests are in the house and is simply the spirits having some fun with those they have come to think of as friends and family. The backstage is also known to give off a weird vibe or energy that seems to be different for each person who senses it. There have also been times when chairs moved on their own; it is believed that this is just another way the spirits show they are still there.

There is another spirit here that has been seen quite often and has become known to not only those who work at the theater but also those in the immediate area. The reason for this notoriety has to do with the belief that this spirit is a former Mafia member who was murdered after it was found out he had been stealing from the mob bosses. The story goes that during the Prohibition era, this person was in charge of picking up illicit booze from the docks and bringing it to the theater. The booze was disguised as stage props, make-up and other theater necessities. Once at the theater, the booze was distributed through the tunnels that linked the various speakeasies and brothels around downtown Ventura that were enjoying a booming business. These tunnels still lie under the streets but are seldom accessed. It would seem that the gangster, thinking his bosses wouldn't miss a bottle or two or a few dollars, decided to skim a bit off the top. The mobster was wrong, deadly

This bloodstain on the cement in the Majestic Theater returns no matter how many times it is scrubbed away.

wrong. Once found out, it didn't take long for him to "sleep with the fishes," and he was shot right there in the theater. It is said that the area where he was shot, now known as the catacombs, has a spot on the concrete floor where his blood emptied out that refuses to be cleaned. Crews will scrub the area until the bloodstain is gone, and when they return, so has the blood.

Across the street from the Majestic Theater lies the Sans Souci Cocktail Lounge. The lounge is connected to the theater by a tunnel, and this was one of the first places the illicit alcohol was sent. No one is sure if the hoodlum's spirit travels between these two places, but the lounge has had reports of phantom footsteps coming from the liquor storage room above the bar to bottles actually levitating while bartenders and guests watch in stunned silence. Many believe that the ghost of the Majestic is also here at the Sans Souci Lounge.

Back at the theater, the ghost of this Mafioso is often seen near the men's restroom on the upper level. This ghost is said to wear a fine pinstriped suit and sports a pencil-thin "Dastardly Dan"–style moustache and will usually be seen smoking a cigarette. As smoking is strictly forbidden in theaters around the country, and especially in California, many folks have approached this spirit to ask him to extinguish his cigarette, only to have him wink, blow smoke in their face, smile and disappear. This ghost has been seen in many areas of the theater, and it would seem that he is a chain smoker, or at least was.

Perhaps the most disturbing spirit found at the Majestic Theater is also the saddest. Over the years, folks touring the theater have seen a girl dressed in a fine white dress, dancing her heart out on stage. As fine a dancer as this girl is, it is not her moves that attract those who watch or keep them from averting their eyes. What captivates the living who espy the spectral dancer aren't her graceful moves but rather her lack of a head. Even though she has no pate, her dance proficiency is never diminished and she never loses

It is not hard to see why so many spirits call the theater home after looking at the luxurious appointments the Majestic offers.

her balance or her steps. No one is certain who this headless ballerina is, but history has it that in the early 1930s, Ventura High School was holding a dance at the theater, and during set up and rehearsal, a few of the girls were horsing around and one of them fell down into what is now the control room. She either broke her neck or had her head removed on the sharp metal stairway. Considering the dancer is sans head, we think we know which may be true. Another story about how this girl came to be headless says that during rehearsal for the prom, a sheet of glass suspended above the young lady came loose, fell and decapitated the woman.

The Ventura/Majestic Theater is one of the most beautiful and historic movie palaces that still stands today and, like its sister the Warner Grand Theater in San Pedro, California, one of the most haunted. Its Spanish revival architecture and Art Deco influences make the Majestic a place everyone should visit. With the beauty of the theater comes a rich history, and with that history comes a plethora of spirits that make this theater in downtown Ventura a must on every ParaTraveler's list of must-see locations. What more could one ask for? History, ghosts and great music in one great location.

10

THE GLEN TAVERN INN

The Santa Clara River Valley is known for its rich farmland and advertises itself as the "Citrus Capital of the World." Some of the finest oranges, lemons and limes come from this region, and just a few miles away sits Rancho Camulos, where the Valencia orange was first grown. The area is also well known for oil, and with the founding of Union Oil Company, which built its headquarters building in Santa Paula, California, this small town would see a growth it never expected, which caught the attention of Hollywood, hookers and gamblers. When the railroad came through, and attention to the town grew, the need for lodgings became paramount. With Hollywood frequenting Santa Paula, that need included upscale accommodations to suit stars' tastes; enter the Glen Tavern Inn.

Built in 1911 directly across from the Santa Paula train depot, the Glen Tavern, built in the Tudor Craftsman style, was designed with the more affluent traveler in mind. Oil tycoons and businessmen, along with visitors sporting upscale tastes, would find just what they were looking for at Glen Tavern, a gathering place for Santa Paula's growing high society. The hotel fared well, but as Prohibition came to pass, the proprietors knew that their wealthy guests would need more "refined" amusements, so the third floor was turned into a speakeasy, gambling hall and brothel. As seems to accompany these types of pastimes, stories of fights between drunken gamblers, shoot-outs, murders and bacchanals filled with all sorts of depravity have come from this time in the inn's history.

The Glen Tavern Inn is not only historic but also extremely haunted.

In the early 1930s, Hollywood, which is relatively close to Santa Paula, discovered the area, and thought it would make a great backdrop for the many westerns it was pumping out, and the Glen Tavern was the inn of choice for Hollywood's elite actors and actresses. Stars such as John Wayne, Harry Houdini, Clark Gable, Carole Lombard and Steve McQueen all walked the halls of this wonderful old inn. Even famed canine actor Rin Tin Tin stayed at the Glen Tavern.

As happens, when the oil became scarce, the railroad stopped less and less at the depot, Hollywood slowed the production of westerns for other genres and the town slowly fell out of favor and memory. As the tourists, businessmen and stars stopped coming to Santa Paula, the Glen Tavern Inn began to decline. When the train depot shut down for good in the early 1960s, the inn struggled to attract guests. With the lack of sufficient funds for proper upkeep, the structure declined until it was unrecognizable as the grand hotel it had once been. It looked like the Glen Tavern Inn would pass into history as have so many other historic inns, but in the late 1970s, a new owner came in and began restoration. In 1981, the Glen Tavern was added to the National Register of Historic Places, and on February 24, 2008, the

Above: The opulent lobby of the Glen Tavern Inn harkens back to its beginnings when catering to the wealthy was its reason for being.

Opposite: The dimly lit hallways of the Glen Tavern may hold more than the ParaTraveler knows.

inn received certificates of special recognition from the U.S. Senate along with the California State Assembly for the restoration of the inn. With its history of Hollywood stars, gambling and prostitution, along with its illicit speakeasy, it is not hard to believe that the Glen Tavern may have a spirit or two walking its well-appointed lobby, dimly lit hallways and comfortable rooms. The Glen Tavern Inn is the most haunted hotel in the whole of the Santa Clara River valley.

"Where the Past Comes to Life" may not be just the Glen Tavern's motto but in fact a reality, for several spirits are known to haunt this historic inn. Most of the reports of spirit activity come from the third floor, but the action is not relegated to that area. One of the more talked-about hauntings is that of a soiled dove by the name of Rose. Rose was one of the more sought-after doves working at the Glen Tavern, and it is thought one of her customers may have been more involved with Rose than she had expected. One evening, after Rose and her would-be suitor had finished their activities, her customer shared his feelings toward her and asked Rose to quit her profession to come away with him. Rose refused, and in a fit of rage, the john murdered Rose by cutting off her head. It is said that the murderer placed Rose's body in the closet and left, hoping that she would not be discovered until long after he was away. Rose was found the next day by a maid coming to check on her.

To this day, those staying in room 307, the room where Rose was killed, have reported a strange mist coming from the closet. Those brave enough to open the closet door find the mist gone the moment it is opened, and no discernable reason for the mist to be emanating from the closet can be found. Many people have heard voices in the room while trying to sleep. The voices sound like a whispered conversation and seem to be coming from the center of the room. When a light is turned on, the voices immediately cease, and all is once again quiet. Areas in the room become suddenly bone-chillingly cold, and knocking is heard along the walls; oftentimes, footsteps can be heard, as if someone is pacing the floor of the room. Another report, albeit rare, is that of the headless apparition of a woman standing in the center of the room. This spirit vanishes from sight just as quickly as it appears. The apparition is usually accompanied by an extreme feeling of despair that washes over the viewer, but the feeling soon goes away when the spirit vanishes.

Another talked about spirit that calls the Glen Tavern home is that of a cowboy named Calvin. This spirit frequents room 308, which happens to now be the hotel's most premium room; it would seem that even in death, Calvin's tastes for refinement haven't changed. Calvin was a gambler and had come to the Glen Tavern to try his luck at the poker tables in the speakeasy. Calvin wasn't very good at poker, but he thought he was good at cheating at cards; sadly, Calvin was wrong. After being caught, Calvin was apparently shot in the head. There seems to be a bit of a discrepancy over whether it was one bullet to his brain or two, but either way, Calvin was dead. According to the Glen Tavern, sometime during restoration, a cowboy hat was found in a crawlspace. The hat had at least one bullet hole through it, along with traces of blood. The hat unfortunately has since disappeared, but could this be proof of Calvin's demise? Regardless, Calvin is well known at the Glen Tavern.

Calvin is said to be a tall, thin man wearing a white shirt and dark pants and sporting long hair and a goatee. Calvin will make his presence known in room 308 by knocking on the walls when one is trying to sleep; this seems to be a frequent occurrence in both of the more haunted rooms and could be one of the spirits that haunts rooms 307 and 308. There have been a number of times where Calvin has been spotted as guests have entered the room; when this happens, Calvin simply nods his head, flashes a smile and fades from view. It would seem that Calvin may have been a cheat, but a cheat with manners. Calvin has also been seen in the lobby of the hotel. He will simply be standing next to the fireplace or walking through as if on his way to the on-property restaurant. Calvin likes to be left alone and seems to be an introverted spirit.

There are a few more spirits that have been reported in the hotel, including a young girl seen running down the hall during restoration work. The workers said they believed the girl was real until they saw her run through the wall. This same girl was reported by a couple staying in room 205. They claim that they saw her late at night, walking through the door into their room and smiling before vanishing. Children have also been heard playing in the hallways and running up and down the stairs while laughing. The *Los Angeles Times* even reported on the spirit of a thirty-four-year-old woman named Helen who wears a "flowery print dress with a white eyelet collar" and a "Buffalo Bill" look-alike who seems to be searching for gold hidden somewhere in the inn's rafters. There is no gold of course, but no one has the heart to tell the spirit this.

Santa Paula, once a thriving, growing city center, is now a sleepy little town nestled in the pristine hills of Ventura County. It is a place where one can come to relax, enjoy the nostalgic small-town Americana atmosphere, walk its quaint downtown and enjoy a slowdown from everyday life. The Glen Tavern is the perfect place to stay to complete the journey. With its Wild West allure, cosmopolitan ambiance and fantastic Italian restaurant, the inn has everything a ParaTraveler needs. Just remember to say hi to its permanent, ghostly residents.

11

RANCHO CAMULOS

Rancho Camulos is a place not many people have heard about, but it has had such an effect on the history of California that it is hard to fathom why it remains in such obscurity. Rancho Camulos is the home of Ramona, the mythical character from Helen Hunt Jackson's famous book *Ramona*, and it's where the very first Valencia orange was grown. Jackson's book was among the driving forces behind the largest migration to the state of California in history. It is also said to be haunted and stalked by an elusive creature of unknown origin.

The rancho began as the Native American village of Kamulus, and in the early 1800s, it became part of the Mission San Fernando Rey de Espania. In 1839, the del Valle family was granted the 48,600-acre San Francisco Rancho; this land grant included the village and all of its lands. Antonio del Valle came to California from Mexico in 1819. As a lieutenant in the Mexican army, he had distinguished himself and was rewarded for his service by the king and queen of Spain personally with one of the largest land grants at the time. After Antonio died in 1841, his son Ygnacio inherited the rancho, expanded it by buying up other lands and became owner of one of the largest land areas in California.

Ygnacio was a good businessman but also a kind man, and he treated his hired hands as well as anyone could expect. To him, they were like family. This became a trait with most of the del Valle family, and their reputation for hospitality became well known throughout California. When Helen Hunt Jackson came to visit the rancho, after only a few short hours of closely observing how things were done and how well those at Camulos were

The Adobe at Rancho Camulos is said to be haunted by several spirits and its grounds plagued by a menacing cryptid.

treated, her mind formed the plot for what would become her most famous literary work, *Ramona*. Although many locations around Southern California claim to be connected with the book, it is only Camulos that has that right. Once the book was released, life at Rancho Camulos would forever change.

Jackson's book was immensely popular in the eastern United States, and with each new reader, the allure of the romanticized California rancho lifestyle grew. People began flocking to the state, and many headed directly for Rancho Camulos, the birthplace and marriage spot for Ramona herself. Camulos's matriarch, Ysabel de Valle, ever the kind hostess, never refused those wishing to stay at the rancho; people would come enjoy food, lodging and wander all over the rancho, and all were accepted warmly by Ysabel and the del Valle family. After a time, it became too much for the family, and with urging, Ysabel had to stop. By that time, however, the influx of people who had moved permanently into California and those who were still on their way had become an unstoppable tidal wave. In 1924, the del Valle family was forced to sell Camulos to a Swiss immigrant by the name of August Rubel. Rubel already owned the nearby Billiwhack Dairy, and his buying of Camulos, along with his dairy, would have lasting and strange effects for the rancho that are still present to this day.

The term *paranormal* does not always mean ghosts and spirits; it sometimes involves strange and unusual creatures. Rancho Camulos does have its fair share of spirits that reside there, but where the ghosts are benign, what August Rubel helped create at his dairy is anything but harmless. It is said that Rubel was approached by the Office of Strategic Services (OSS) in the time leading up to America's entry into World War II. The OSS was the precursor to today's CIA, and the organization asked Rubel if it could use his dairy for research into different types of unusual weapons. Rubel, being the patriot that he was for his adopted country, agreed; he also joined the OSS as an operative. Over the intervening years, the OSS brought captured Axis soldiers to the underground labs below the dairy and experimented on them, looking for ways to develop a "super soldier." One wonders if the OSS had read too many Captain America comic books, but regardless of what the service attempted to create, what came out of these experiments was a creature devoid of reason, thought or regard for human life. What it did possess was great strength, size, longevity and a will to be free—and stay that way. After it had escaped captivity, the locals began seeing this creature roaming not only the countryside but sometimes in towns and farms as well; it became known as the Billiwhack Monster.

The first indication that something strange was afoot in the area of the Santa Clara River Valley came in the early 1950s when a nine-year-old boy came rushing home to tell his parents that he had been attacked and had barely escaped from "a strange creature." The parents saw the boy had scratch marks all over his arms and back; he also looked more frightened than they had ever seen him. Even though the police and a large group of townsfolk scoured the countryside, no sign of a creature was found. After the incident with the boy, reports began to flood in of rocks as heavy as sixty pounds being lobbed at cars; farm animals gone missing, with other accounts of their half-eaten remains being found in pastures; and even a few instances of a creature that looked like a cross between a giant man and a goat approaching cars, smashing hoods, trunks and side doors.

In the early 1960s, the reports of this goat-man became so widespread that the *Los Angeles Times* wrote a featured article about the Billiwhack Monster. The article talks about a young boy being picked up by police for walking around carrying a large sword. It seems the child was intent on "slaying the beast" and getting a reward. Another story in the news article claims that a large group of "Billiwhack hunting" children were detained by a resident with a shotgun until the police arrived to take them home. No mention was made of whether the police talked to the woman about pulling a shotgun on a bunch of kids.

Strange mists are seen floating down the walkways of the old adobe.

Another news report from 1964 claims that a group of hikers had been stalked by a strange and menacing-looking hairy creature. The hikers said that it followed them for a few hours but never got close enough for them to figure out exactly what it might be. A few in the group figured it was a bear but couldn't understand why the bear would stalk them in an upright position for as long as it had.

Whether the Billiwhack Monster is real or a case of prolonged mass hysteria remains to be seen, but to this day, reports of this creature are made to police stations and 911 dispatchers at least once a month. August Rubel was killed in Tunisia, supposedly in a convoy accident while on a mission for the OSS. Many believe this to be nothing more than a cover story due to the OSS eliminating a witness to the creature and its escape. We may never know the truth of these tales, but if the reports of Rubel being eliminated are to be believed, it may be why Rubel still haunts Rancho Camulos to this day.

The Billiwhack Monster is said to have been created here at the Billiwhack Dairy.

Rubel has been seen at the ranch house on many occasions. Even if he is not seen, he makes his presence known by an oppressive feeling that comes over anyone nearby, and there have been times when his name is mentioned out loud that a voice will call out, "Do not speak about Rubel." Edwin Burger, Mary Rubel's second husband, is also said to haunt Rancho Camulos. Burger was always a solitary man, and when anyone enters the room where Burger slept and died, it can elicit a feeling of wanting to be left alone; this feeling will pass but only when leaving the room. A shadowy figure has also been seen in this room, but unlike what people normally call a shadow figure, one can clearly make out the features of a man. It is believed that this is Edwin Burger going about his daily life as if he doesn't realize he has passed away.

In the upstairs area of the adobe, people have reported being lightly shoved while at the same time hearing their name called out in a whispered voice. Strange noises have been heard coming from the upper area even though there was no one present, and the sounds of footsteps, things being moved around and other sounds of what could be called "living life" have come from all over the adobe. It sometimes seems as if those who once dwelled at the rancho are still going about their day-to-day lives as if nothing has changed for them. Who knows? For them it may not have changed. There are other areas of the house and grounds where activity takes place; the chapel is known to emit strange EVPs, the library of the adobe is said to have books move on their own and the bedroom that was once the nursery is said to have the sounds of children at play and emit a warm and safe feeling to those with the "gift."

Rancho Camulos is a museum and wedding and event venue with wonderful gardens and fountains. The museum hosts events for the community and anyone else who would like to attend, along with many

Ramona-related festivals. Art shows, picnics, historical tours of the grounds and adobe as well as sanctioned ghost hunts all add to the beauty and welcoming atmosphere of this historic yet all but forgotten piece of California's growth as a state. It is almost as if Ysabel del Valle is still welcoming guests with her kindness and hospitality to this day; of course, she most likely is.

12
CAMARILLO STATE MENTAL HOSPITAL

C amarillo State Mental Hospital is not that well known, even in California. Those who do know the name sometimes associate the place with the song "Hotel California" by the Eagles, while others may only know it by its new name, Channel Islands State University. For those of us who know its past, its history of pain and torture, it is something much more. Camarillo was once one of the most barbaric mental hospitals in the country and perhaps the world. Its history of wet electroshock, routine lobotomies and sensory deprivation treatments was both cruel and unusual, and this hospital was anything but humane.

Camarillo became so big that it grew to become its own small town, with a neighborhood of houses for its staff. It had a farm and dairy that supplied not only the hospital but also the town of Camarillo. With a municipal electric and sewer grid, this hospital was not only self-sustaining but also remote enough to not raise suspicions about what was actually going on within its walls. Much of the labor was supplied by the more docile patients, and there were many who hoped that the labor and trade development would prepare them for life outside of the asylum walls. For those patients deemed unruly, insane or beyond help, life inside those same walls could be a living hell. Lobotomies became a commonplace "cure"; electroshock treatments with the added suffering of being immersed in water, locked in a pitch-black room with no sound and only one's thoughts, could and would drive patients on the cusp of lucidity mad. Those who may have been on the edge of irreversible insanity were driven deeper into the abyss of their own

The historic bell tower at California State University Channel Islands shows the Spanish influence the old mental hospital was built to resemble.

minds. Camarillo was truly something out of a horror movie. The hospital was finally shuttered for good on June 30, 1997, not for mistreatment of patients but for the cost of keeping it open.

With all of the terrors that took place at this supposed hospital, it is not surprising to find that it is one of the most haunted asylums in the country— or would have been if the whole area hadn't been turned into a place of higher learning. Many of the original buildings have been placed on the National Register of Historic Places; this saved them from destruction, and they were turned into classrooms. As someone who has investigated many, if not all of these areas once used for patient housing and knows just how haunted they are, I have to wonder if the students at Channel Islands State University have trouble concentrating in class. I also wonder if those in the dorms, which are directly next to the old hospital wards, have their very own ghostly tutors to help them with their studies.

Over the years, many people have reported hearing the laughter of children and voices of the young at play. This occurs in many areas around the campus but most frequently in the area once designated as the children's ward. This area is well known for spectral children at play in what was once a fenced-in play yard. There is no longer a fence or any playground equipment, but the kids are often seen riding a merry-go-round or a teeter-totter. The view is, shall we say, unnerving at best. Camarillo Hospital is and always was one of those places that ghost hunters and ParaTravelers alike have sought out. Over the years, many apparitions have been glimpsed looking out of empty rooms, sometimes staring at those outside, at other times simply staring out into space, seemingly lost in thought or dreaming of life outside the hospital walls. There are times, however, when those looking out have an obvious insanity about their visage and what looks like murder in their eyes. Those visiting Camarillo would be wise to not stare long but move away, just in case. Those who have gone inside these old wards have found what looks like unoccupied rooms and corridors; however, this is not always the case. There have been many reports of phantom figures moving about these rooms, and folks have told tales about objects moving with no explanation as to why. Some things roll down the hallways—items that should not move on their own—topsy-turvy toward those who watch their movement. There are reports of folks claiming to walk into a room and have a sudden feeling of panic wash over them, only to have it dispelled as fast as it came the moment they walk back out the door. There have been times when figures that seem as big as giants have suddenly appeared in front of a group of ghost hunters to menace them and fade once the "interlopers" have left the ward.

Abundant EVPs have been caught in many places inside and out—but mostly in the wards where patients were housed. On many occasions, these EVPs will have desperate voices calling out for help, and at other times, the voices are pleading for someone to stop doing whatever it is that the spirit perceives is happening to them. One EVP captured at Camarillo State Hospital is of a patient who, in response to a derogatory tone from an investigator, used the same disparaging voice to call the offending ghost hunter "an asshole."

Just down the road from the university is a dirt lane that leads to what many have come to call the "Scary Dairy." This area is accessible only by foot or motorcycle and has earned its nickname from many years of both ghost stories and motorcycle gangs. The motorcycle gangs have been mainly eliminated; the ghosts, however, seem to call the place home. Here you will find a barn that is said to have the spirit of a patient who died by hanging from the rafters. This spirit is known for calling out the names of those who wander near and will try to beckon them into the barn. No

This dorm room, once part of the hospital's women's ward, has caused many ghost hunters to have panic attacks until they leave the room.

one is sure why this spirit wants them in the barn, but to this day no one has ever admitted to following the ghost's plea. If you venture a bit past the barn, you will come to the dairy itself. Now closed off by a chain-link fence, the Scary Dairy is said to be the most haunted spot at Camarillo and perhaps the entire Ventura area. Many folks who have come to the dairy have said so many ghosts occupy the series of buildings that it is hard not to find one if you look. People have claimed to hear their names called, heard footsteps following them and seen shadows wandering all over the complex. There have even been reports of menacing shadow figures chasing folks away. Other people claim to smell rotten milk, cheese and other rancid dairy products. There have even been the occasional reports of the wafting stench of a "wet cow."

A few other strange things about Camarillo State Hospital are a road leading to the back of the campus that seems to have more than its share of

The Scary Dairy near the old mental hospital is said to be the most haunted area of the asylum.

accidents and mists that move around the grounds defying the direction of the wind. There are even reports about catching the scents of a hospital that no longer exists.

Say what you will about old Camarillo State Hospital, for those of us who have been there and investigated there, we have no doubts that it is truly haunted. Let's just hope that the students who live and learn on the campus of Channel Islands University know what they got themselves into by enrolling in one of the most haunted schools in the world.

13

SPAHN RANCH

Charles Manson may be one of the evilest men to have ever lived. To many, he ranks up there with the likes of Hitler, Stalin and Pol Pot. To others, he has become a folk hero and leader. He committed a murder as a child in reform school and, as an adult, persuaded his followers to do the deed for him. At times, Manson watched, and he taught them how it should be done. And then there are others who believe him to be innocent of the crimes and that he should never have been tried or convicted. The one thing we know for certain is that Manson not only allowed his followers to commit some of the most violent and gruesome murders in history, but he also ordered them to do it. Crimes such as those the Manson Family perpetrated are never forgotten. Their heinous deeds have left an indelible scar on history and a legacy of ghosts and torment on the place where they lived in the Santa Susana Mountains of Southern California, a placed called Spahn Ranch.

Spahn Ranch was an old western movie ranch when Manson and his followers moved in, rent free, by providing sex, work and other benefits to eighty-year-old George Spahn. It was Spahn who gave Lynette Fromme the nickname "Squeaky" due to the sounds she would make while they were having sex. One wonders if Spahn, regardless of the endless sex he was promised, would have given the Family safe haven if he had known what they were planning or of Manson's hatred for his hired hand Donald "Shorty" Shea. Many know about the ghosts of Sharon Tate and the others who were killed by Manson, but few know about the ghosts that still linger

The Manson Cave, as it has come to be called, is where *Time* magazine snapped a photo of the Manson family for the cover of the magazine. *Courtesy of Gerald Reynolds.*

at what remains of Spahn Ranch or the dark omen, known as the Watcher, that keeps folks from stopping along the roadway in front of the ranch.

Manson and Shea did not get along the entire time the Family lived at the ranch. Shorty knew that Manson was only using his boss and friend George Spahn, and even though Shea was loyal to his boss and would never have turned Manson and his Family in to authorities, Manson believed that is exactly what Shea had done. Because of this belief, Manson ordered Tex Watson, Bruce Davis and Steve Grogan to murder Shorty, so that is what his brainwashed followers did, violently and with malice. Shea was beaten with a hammer, stabbed and tortured for a crime he never committed. This all happened under the tree next to the road where Manson took his followers to play the guitar and sing to them; to this day, the tree is known as the Manson Tree. Shorty was buried by the railroad tracks near the ranch, where his body was finally found in 1977. As brutal as Shea's death had been, the former stuntman and ranch hand couldn't bear to leave his boss or the ranch and remains there still.

Donald "Shorty" Shea is often seen standing atop a hill that overlooks both the ranch or what is left of it and the place where he was murdered. When seen, Shorty will simply stand there looking around and then slowly

Inside this culvert is where Shorty Shea suffered for hours while slowly dying after the attack by Manson followers.

fade from view. No one has yet been able to determine what Shorty is looking for, though many believe he is looking for those who killed him or perhaps his old boss, George Spahn. Shorty has also been seen walking through the area where the buildings of the old movie town once stood. Time and the elements have almost completely erased the town, but Shea is sometimes seen working on structures that no longer exist. It is a testament to Shorty's work ethic and dedication to Spahn that even in death he still works around the ranch.

There are also reports from many folks who have seen a headless man standing in plain view near the area where Shea has been seen. No one knows who this other person may be, but some believe this to be Shorty as well. There was a rumor that Shorty was beheaded and dismembered when he was killed; where the rumor began is unknown and unimportant, but it was completely dispelled when the man's completely intact body was finally discovered.

Other spirits have been seen wandering around the site of the old movie ranch and the area known as the Manson Cave. This cave was where *Time* magazine held a photoshoot with the members of the Family, including those who would commit the brutal murders. Maybe it was the photoshoot that draws some of the deceased Manson Family back to the cave, for that is who most folks believe the spirits seen here are, or it could be some of the victims the Family claimed over the years before the notorious murders. We may never know the answer.

Another odd thing that people report near the Spahn Ranch are the sounds of crying infants. While the Manson clan was living at the ranch, sex—or free love, as it was called—was common and so were pregnancies. There is a cave a little way south from where the ranch once stood, and this small cave was sometimes used as a nursery or place to keep the children quiet while Manson was sleeping or didn't want to be disturbed. As many hear the crying while walking along the highway, it may be this now lost cave that the crying is coming from.

There is another strange thing that happens in front of the Spahn Ranch and only while passersby are driving down the road. Many folks will be just about to pass in front of the ranch site when a deep, male laugh will suddenly come across the car radio, even if it is turned off. Then, shortly afterward, the Watcher will appear. With the sound of a revving engine, a quick glance in the rearview mirror will show a black 1960s sedan speeding up to tailgate the unsuspecting motorist. If the driver speeds up, the sedan speeds up; if the driver pulls over and stops, the sedan does as well—it is one of those things

Under this tree, Manson would sing to his followers. Shorty Shea was murdered here and suffered an agonizing death.

that frightens you no matter who you are. No one ever gets out of the old car, and no one can be seen behind the wheel due to dirt covering the windshield. However, in every instance, as soon as the unsuspecting driver passes the old Manson compound at the ranch, the black car suddenly vanishes as quickly and mysteriously as it appeared. No one knows who the Watcher is or why he seems to guard the Spahn Ranch. Because the sedan is obviously a 1960s model and always appears near the Manson Family hideout, many think it is somehow connected to the Manson Family and is trying to keep interlopers away from their guru and messiah Charles Manson.

Today, the Spahn Ranch is almost completely lost to time. The only things left of the town are bits and pieces of machinery, some scraps of junk and the Manson Cave. The rest is lost now, remembered only by history and those who won't or can't forget the brutal crimes of those who once lived here. One of the saddest things about the old ranch are those many new followers of Manson who make a pilgrimage to the site in the hopes of gleaning some new knowledge or insight from the man to whom they have become devoted. Manson has more acolytes now than he had before the heinous crimes he and his followers committed. Let us hope that these new lost and confused souls don't sink so deep that history repeats itself or that we allow it to happen again.

14

UNIVERSAL STUDIOS, HOLLYWOOD

U niversal Studios may have begun as a relatively small film company on the East Coast, but it has grown into one of the premier Hollywood movie studios and become a worldwide amusement park venue with theme parks spread all over the globe. It was Universal Studios that gave us the iconic look of Count Dracula, the flat-headed and bolt-ridden profile of Frankenstein's Monster, the rag-dragging Mummy and the gilled and lovelorn Creature from the Black Lagoon. Who could forget the iconic and horrifying Phantom of the Opera Lon Chaney and Universal Studios released on an unsuspecting world? Without Universal Studios, the monster pantheon that we know and love would look much different than it does today. With the history of Universal Studios came many firsts, many stars and crew who came to love the limelight and didn't want to give them up after death. This may be one of the main reasons that Universal Studios Hollywood could be the most haunted theme park in the world.

Carl Laemmle was a diminutive man with a big dream. Coming from Germany, Carl found solace in the films he watched and thought how grand it would be to create movies. After seeing folks hand over their money at nickelodeons and with his love of films, Laemmle opened up his own small studio. Unfortunately, this angered Thomas Edison, who had cornered the market on films and distribution. After a long and drawn-out court battle, Laemmle won, and Hollywood history was about to be made.

After setting up a film studio in New Jersey, Laemmle knew that he would need to grow to become the successful moviemaker he had always dreamed

Universal Studios, Hollywood, is the only amusement park where you can see your favorite movie stars, alive or dead, walking the back lot.

of becoming. Knowing that the film industry was set to make a boom out on the West Coast, Carl purchased a large piece of land and built what would become the largest and, at the time, most profitable studio the world had ever seen. Not in Hollywood, but close enough that folks could come and watch their stars and idols film the movies they loved, Carl found that folks flocked to his studio to see the magic being made. He encouraged his guests to cheer their heroes and boo the bad guys, and everyone involved—crew, stars and spectators—loved every minute of it. That was, until talkies came on the scene. Once sound was introduced, it became a serious problem trying to get the crowds of onlookers to keep quiet while the cameras were rolling, and the studio was forced to shut out the fans.

As the years passed and the technology of movie making improved, Universal once again tried allowing movie fans to come to the studio. With guided tours and off-limits filming areas, the new studio attraction was a huge hit. With fans still eager to see where the movies were made, Universal created the now famous Studio Backlot tour. Once folks started to come back to Universal Studios, there was no stopping them, and today Universal Studios parks are among the most popular amusement parks in the world. The difference between all of the other parks and the one in Hollywood is that the original is the only one where you can still see your favorite movie star and the only one with a backlot tour. It is also the only one where you may just run into your favorite movie star who is no longer with us in life.

From the second day of the studio's grand opening in 1915, a spirit has made Universal its home. Frank Stites, a stunt pilot and barnstormer, ran into trouble during his stunt meant to wow Laemmle's guests during the grand opening. Stites, not waiting for his plane to crash, jumped from the stricken craft and was killed; his story should have ended there. However, years later, it seems that Stites has remained at the studio near the place he perished.

One night while a producer and his assistant were roaming around the area near the Psycho House looking for places to extend the park's popular Halloween Horror Nights event, they heard the sound of giggling. The producer knew that he and his assistant were the only ones in that section of the backlot, and even though the giggle only lasted a minute or so, the frightening tone of the laughter caused him to flee the area. His assistant had to convince the producer to come back, which took a while, but then just as he returned, the giggling sounded again, only this time much closer to them. Both he and his assistant fled from the area, and neither returned that evening.

The next day, quite a few people told the producer that they had seen a figure wearing a vintage pilot uniform with an old-style leather flight helmet wandering around in the same location that he had heard the giggling. The producer began asking other employees about this pilot, and it turned out that this spirit has been seen for a very long time in the area. Thinking this was possibly an actual spirit lurking in the backlot, the producer began to research any deaths that may have taken place during filming or any other reason that a man in a pilot suit would be stalking the backlot. What he found was a *Los Angeles Times* article dated March 17, 1915, about the opening days of Universal City and the death of Stites.

Thinking that Frank Stites might be hanging out in the backlot of the studio in order to not be forgotten, the producer went to the prop department, grabbed a mannequin, went over to wardrobe and from the discards section gathered up enough pieces of costume to create a passable version of a 1915-style aviator's uniform. The producer then took the effigy to the area where the activity was reported and put it as close as possible to the spot where Frank Stites's body had landed. After the mannequin was in place, the director said a few words to Stites, letting him know that he would be remembered. Since the effigy has been in place, no more giggling has been heard, and the specter of Frank Stites hasn't been seen—well, mostly. If someone inadvertently moves the effigy, Frank will reappear until the mannequin is replaced. So, if you see Frank, let the staff at Universal know.

Many actors and actresses love their craft and their fans so much that they simply don't want to leave or let them down. This may be the case with a few well-known actors who owe much of their careers to Universal Studios. One such is none other than *Phantom of the Opera* star Lon Chaney. Lon is known to still be hanging around the opera set that made him more famous than he ever imagined, sound stage 28.

Sound stage 28 used to be a part of the backlot tram tour, and for those who wanted to get a glimpse of the actual stage, Universal used to give tours of the building for guests to get a peek at the famous opera house set and view some of the areas where the stars would get ready for their upcoming movie shoots. Quite a few folks would ask the tour guides if it was true that Lon Chaney haunted the sound stage; they would always tell them yes. Chaney was often seen in the sound stage by movie and TV crews getting ready for an upcoming shoot. He was usually seen up on the catwalks strolling along for unknown reasons. He was often seen in full Phantom regalia and on occasion carrying a chandelier (most likely they mean candelabra). I say *was*, because unfortunately sound stage 28, one of the oldest sound stages at Universal, was torn down to make way for rides in the lower lot section of the amusement park. It would seem, however, that Chaney may still be haunting the area where the sound stage once stood and has since been seen in the rides that took its place.

Lon Chaney is not the only star known to have come back to Universal Studios. Lucille Ball has been seen walking from where her dressing room used to be to the sound stage across the way, and Alfred Hitchcock is said to have monitored Steven Spielberg's work to the point that Spielberg had to move from the office that was once Hitchcock's. From movie stars and directors to producers and crew, Universal Studios is still home to dedicated filmmakers who have not given up the ghost for movie fans.

It is not only the backlot and studio areas of Universal where spirits remain but also the amusement park and CityWalk as well. The lower lot, where sound stage 28 used to be, is a hotbed for paranormal activity. Here you will find an ice cream stand that seems to have a spirit with not only a sweet tooth but also a mischievous nature. This spirit likes to move things around in the freezer and sometimes closes the freezer door on employees. There is the phantom scare actor who is so good that the living cast of Hollywood Horror Nights working the lower lot have actually come to

If you look closely at the upper window of the original Psycho House, you can catch a glimpse of "Mother" peeking back at you.

admire his skill and a phantom who some believe to be a former guest who likes to play late-night hide-and-seek with the security guards once the park has closed. But perhaps the most well-known and playful spirit of the lower lot is that of a young girl.

The Jurassic Outfitters store is directly adjacent to Jurassic Park: The Ride, and people exiting this ride must walk through the souvenir store. It is here that a young girl likes to hang out. One employee said that she was working, and there were only a few patrons left in the store when she saw a little girl wandering around. This girl seemed to be about nine years old and looked lost; as the employee didn't see an adult with the child, she approached her. As the store clerk neared, the girl shook her head and disappeared.

Another clerk told me that a strange mist came out of nowhere and became so thick that it completely obscured the view of everything beyond the doorway. It lingered for a couple of minutes, and then, just as the fog was about to completely disappear, she heard a giggle and all of the merchandise on the shelves near where the mist had been flew off the shelves and landed on the floor. It would seem that this girl has a penchant for the dramatic, which suits Universal Studios well.

The upper lot has its own mischievous little girl who likes to play tricks on the living. She is often seen in and near the Simpsons Ride and the store out front. However, where this little girl is playful, there is another spirit that is anything but. A few years past, a man died by suicide in front of Los Angeles sheriff's deputies rather than go to jail for harassing his girlfriend. Today, this man is seen near the area where he took his life and, more disturbing, in and around the children's area of the park, near where he did the deed.

Perhaps the most amusing spirits, unless you are one of the employees, is the ghost in the Production Central Store. According to the clerks I spoke with, they were helping guests when one of them noticed that the mannequin in the store had been moved. It should have been facing the front of the shop but was now turned, facing the back wall. The clerk moved it back and forgot all about it. About ten minutes later, he found that it had again been moved to face the back of the store. He thought someone was playing with them but figured that if he paid attention he would catch the culprit. A while later, his co-worker saw the mannequin was once again facing backward. Both said they had been keeping a close eye for the last hour or so and hadn't seen anyone messing with it. As the two watched, the mannequin began rotating back to where it was supposed to be facing, and they bolted for the door.

From Chocolate Frogs jumping off of the shelves in the Harry Potter Store to employees getting locked in storage rooms, the upper lot has more fun in store for visitors than just the rides and walk-through attractions.

It is not only Universal Studios that is haunted. The area one must walk through to get from the parking lot to the park entrance is said to be haunted as well. This area is known as CityWalk, and it is basically a mall with shops, eateries and other retail stores. It also has a few nightclubs, and many of the spirits here have come from these, or so it is believed. One

The Simpsons Ride, and Krusty's, just outside of the ride, have a spectral little girl who enjoys playing with the staff and guests.

of these is a spirit seen running down the mall thoroughfare. The story goes that the LAPD, responding to a disturbance, arrived to find a large group of people being a nuisance outside the Infusion Lounge nightclub. When the officers approached, shots rang out, and everyone took cover. The officers ordered the shooter to drop the gun but were forced to fire when the young man didn't respond, killing him. Since that night, there have been reports of a spirit running down the wide boardwalk near where the young man was killed.

One of the stranger hauntings comes from the women's restroom behind the Raider Store and just as you exit the parking lot into CityWalk itself. It seems that the spirit here is not content to let the ladies have their privacy while using the loo. With the Hard Rock Store and the prolific haunts of the wonderful Mexican restaurant Antojito's (formerly Camacho's), one doesn't need to enter Universal Studios to get a ghost fix. CityWalk can be just as spectral, although no proper ParaTraveler would dare miss out on all that Universal has to offer in the way of fun and movie spirits.

15

THELMA TODD'S CAFÉ

Thelma Todd was a rare beauty and a woman who had plenty of talent to go along with her looks. She had a comedic flare that made her a favorite with movie audiences and also made her a favorite with those in the movie industry. Dramatic roles were just as easy for her as comedy, and the best directors of the time, such as Hal Roach and Roland West, were just as eager to have her in their pictures as the premier comedy stars were to have her in theirs. She was a rising star in an era when Hollywood was about to become the main venue of entertainment around the world. Alas, the stars that burn the brightest are those that flicker and go out the quickest—or so the proverb tells us.

Thelma Todd garnered the nickname of "Hot Toddy" among her peers and the moviegoing public. This was partly due to her social life and partly due to folks thinking she was one of the most beautiful women to grace the screen in the early days of Hollywood. Her movie career looked like it would continue well into the mid-twentieth century; unfortunately, Thelma Todd's love life would not be so lucky. In 1932, Todd married well-known "gigolo" Pasquale "Pat" DiCicco. Thelma, however, either couldn't see the truth or didn't care that her new husband was a womanizer, or her marriage could have been a ploy to make the man she was in love with, director Roland West, jealous. West had rejected her advances after her admission to being in love with the much older man. Thelma made sure to be seen with DiCicco and went out of her way to be places with him she knew West frequented. Unfortunately, after moving into the chateau-style Villa Celia apartments,

Thelma and Pat began fighting almost every night. The neighbors began complaining and threatening to call the police. It wasn't long before Todd's husband begun to physically abuse her, and his abuse got worse as time went on. One night while coming home from the Coconut Grove, Pat drove off the road in a fit of rage, and Thelma suffered a broken shoulder that delayed the start of her new film. While she recovered in the hospital, she made up her mind to leave DiCicco as soon as possible. As soon as Thelma recovered enough to begin production on the movie *The Devil's Brother*, she was offered a role in a new Laurel and Hardy comedy. When this movie was finished, Hal Roach sent the stars of the picture to London on a promotional tour. Todd was more than happy to be away from her abusive husband. While on this tour, she was offered a role in the film *You Made Me Love You* starring Stanley Lupino, which was being shot in England. As this would mean even more time away from home and the abusive DiCicco, Thelma readily agreed to appear in the film. While in Europe, Thelma was diagnosed with a heart condition, and because her father had died of a heart attack, this convinced her even more to end her marriage as soon as she returned home.

By the time Thelma Todd's divorce was finalized in 1934, she had partnered with Roland West, the man she was still in love with, to open up an

Thelma Todd's Café has gone through many owners since the starlet passed away but still stands on Pacific Coast Highway to this day.

upscale café along Pacific Coast Highway in the chic beach town of Malibu, California. This venture, at least for the "Ice Cream Blonde" as Todd was now being called, had two purposes. The first was to make sure that Thelma had a steady income when her movie career began to decline as age crept up on her. Thelma was an intelligent woman who knew that Hollywood was fickle and parts would start to decline as she grew older. Second, Thelma, knowing West was married and had already spurned her advances, wanted an excuse to be near the man she would always love.

Thelma Todd's Café opened directly across from Pacific Palisades Beach and catered to the rich and famous of Hollywood and beyond. The restaurant had two levels: a casual yet upscale café on the lower level and a more luxurious, reservations-only fine-dining restaurant on the second floor. While the first floor was almost always filled to capacity with tourists hoping to catch a glimpse of the "Hot Toddy," the upper room, named Joya's Room, hosted Hollywood's elite along with the rich and famous from all over the country and the world. Celebrities such as Laurel and Hardy, Walt Disney, Joe E. Brown and Gloria Swanson were regulars, and the two partners knew almost immediately that the café was going to be a great success.

Roland West lived directly behind the café, up a long, steep stairway, and Thelma Todd moved into the third floor of the café building. Roland's wife, Jewel, had suffered a nervous breakdown and spent almost all of her time at the house recovering. She was also suspicious of the relationship between Thelma and her husband. Thelma Todd was still considered a party girl and would go out to the clubs most nights but was never seen in the company of other men. Jewel also knew that her husband and Thelma went out on West's yacht, the MV *Joyita*, for long weekends over to Catalina Island. To Jewel, this all added up to one thing. It would all come to a sad end on December 16, 1935.

Thelma owned a Lincoln Phaeton that was her pride and joy. West allowed her to keep it in his garage, as he had plenty of room. Roland, his wife and a few of Thelma's close friends became worried about her, as she hadn't been seen since she had been dropped off after a party on Saturday night. Around 9:30 a.m. on December 16, 1935, Mae Whitehead, Thelma's housekeeper and maid, arrived at the garage to make sure Thelma's Lincoln was ready to go, just as she did every weekday. When she opened the garage, she saw that the car's driver's side door was ajar, and as she walked up to inspect the car, she saw the body of Thelma, slumped down behind the wheel with her head resting on the seat. She still wore the clothes she had worn to the Trocadero Nightclub two days before, and it was obvious that she was dead. The aftermath of Thelma's death has since been mired in controversy, conspiracy theories and Hollywood legend. The final coroner's report listed accidental death by carbon monoxide poisoning. Regardless of all of the hype over her death, Thelma Todd was nevertheless dead, and the world had lost a rising star and beautiful soul.

One of the theories put forth about her death has to do with a meeting between Lucky Luciano and Thelma at the café. It is said that Luciano came out to strong-arm Todd into turning over Joya's Room to the mob as an illicit gambling hall; when Thelma refused, Luciano had her killed. One problem with this theory is that Luciano never set foot in California, let alone Thelma Todd's Café. Another theory is that West killed Thelma while out on an early morning cruise after the party Thelma had attended, then placed her body in the Lincoln Phaeton to make it look like an accident. This could be the reason that West's yacht, the MV *Joyita*, was forever cursed after Thelma Todd's death. (For more on the curse of the MV *Joyita*, read my book, *Hollywood Obscura*.) With so many stories going around, not only regarding her death but also about the "Hot Toddy" herself, these tales might be the reason Miss Todd has not been able to find peace in the afterlife.

After Thelma's death, the café was sold several times and has had many uses, from simple office space to a Christian TV studio. The one thing that hasn't changed since her death is that Thelma is still there. Many people who have worked in the building have claimed to see Thelma Todd quite often. She is usually seen walking down the stairs and will sometimes make her way to the outside courtyard. Folks who have seen her in the courtyard say she seems confused. She will stand there for a few moments, glide toward Pacific Coast Highway and vanish. She is sometimes seen exiting the stairs to wander through what was once the lower café, stopping from time to time as if pausing at a table, repeating this a few times, seemingly making her rounds for the tourists she believes still come to enjoy her café.

Upstairs, where the more private, high-class café Joya's once stood, Thelma has been seen making the rounds of the now nonexistent tables as she does in the lower cafe. The main difference is that when she is seen in Joya's, she is usually dressed in an evening gown, and even though her appearance is wispy, one can tell that she is dressed to impress her Hollywood friends. She has also been seen on the third floor. As this area used to be her private apartment, she is often seen lounging on a spectral couch or chair, simply relaxing and enjoying being out of the limelight. Todd has been seen pacing the floor, almost as if waiting for something, and is wearing casual clothes of the style worn in the 1930s. She has even been seen wearing a nightgown

This garage, where Thelma Todd died, is said to be haunted by a spectral Lincoln Phaeton automobile.

and robe on more than one occasion. It would seem that Thelma is just as comfortable in her sidewalk café in death as she was while she was alive.

Thelma Todd has also been seen walking around near the stone steps that lead up from the highway. It was here that she had been dropped off to make her way up to the café. It is said that Thelma used to love to walk across to the beach and has even been seen walking across the old pedestrian bridge that still today allows folks to safely cross Pacific Coast Highway. Her spirit is always seen late at night by lovers and others who are still on the beach and drivers just passing under the bridge.

Another place where Thelma Todd is often seen and felt is the garage where her body was found. Over the years, visitors coming to the spot Thelma died have reported walking up to the garage and hearing the sound of a car; even if the door is open and no car can be seen, the sound of the engine is clear as day. Residents who live at the mansion today have reported the same thing at all hours of the day and night. They have said that the sound of a car idling in the garage has become so frequent that they no longer go down to check whether they had left their own vehicle running by mistake. Even though the sound can be heard at any time, they say it seems to be more frequent around the hours of 3:00 to 4:00 a.m., the same hours that Thelma would have been there trying to stay warm the night she died. Other reports coming from the garage are people smelling carbon monoxide, the deadly gas that comes from car exhaust fumes. People have reported that the gas fumes have become so overwhelming they made them sick, prompting some to leave the area for fear of passing out. The fumes are noticeable even when there is no sound of an engine running or even a car in the garage or anywhere in the area.

Many people have heard about "Thelma Todd's Garage" regarding her spirit still lurking about, but few have explored the tales about her old café. This may have to do with it being mostly closed off to the public since her death or perhaps due to the Christian influence that the old café has been under for so many years. Whatever the case may be, it seems clear that Thelma still has unfinished business that keeps her on this side of the veil. For those ParaTravelers who come to look for the "Ice Cream Blonde," remember that both the garage and the building where the café once stood are still private property and be respectful of those who own them. Who knows, you just may see Thelma walking around the old café, or the beautiful Hot Toddy may just visit you while walking across to dip your feet into the blue Pacific.

16

COLORADO STREET (SUICIDE) BRIDGE

Another haunted location that happens to be on old Route 66 is the Colorado Street Bridge, more commonly called the Suicide Bridge. This bridge is perhaps one of the grandest of design in the state, and its elegance and beauty belie the deadly history that began almost from the day it was opened in 1913—perhaps even before it was erected. Today, maybe because the bridge is so high above the Arroyo Seco or due to its nearness to what is called Devil's Gate Dam, the Suicide Bridge must be constantly watched for those wanting to end their lives. It has also become a magnet for ghost hunters and ParaTravelers alike. For you see, the Colorado Street Suicide Bridge has a highly haunted reputation.

The first ghost stories involving the bridge began almost from the day the span opened to traffic. There is a tale about a construction worker who fell to his death and landed in wet cement that had just been poured into its forms. Since the worker was dead and removing his body would result in the ruination of the fresh cement, he was left in the forms to become a permanent part of the bridge. This story seems to pop up where construction and cement are used, and most, if not all, involve a ghost. Of course, if this happened to me, I would most certainly haunt the site of my demise.

The Colorado Street Bridge was built with a pedestrian walkway, and right after the bridge opened, those walking across began to hear a voice calling, "Look out," and "Hurry and get off the bridge." It is believed that this spirit is John Visco, the man who allegedly died falling off the span into the wet cement trying to warn people of the impending scaffolding

The height of the majestic Colorado Street Bridge is almost a guarantee of death for those wishing to do themselves harm.

collapse that caused his death. Locals and visitors walking across the bridge have also reported seeing the apparition of a woman in a white gown leaping from a parapet. Just before the lady jumps, she will glance over at onlookers, leap and then vanish while in midair. Yet another spirit commonly seen by those walking along the bridge is that of a man wearing wire-rimmed glasses and a suit who simply wanders back and forth along the bridge, seemingly in a daze.

As haunted as the bridge is, the Arroyo Seco directly under the span may be even more haunted than the bridge itself. This, of course, is due to the jumpers from the span itself, so the bridge and arroyo have a symbiotic relationship with the paranormal in this regard. Many of those walking on and below the bridge, along with those living nearby, have reported seeing wispy silhouettes walking among the trees and bushes, and many have heard the sound of a woman screaming as if she has jumped from the heights above. The scream will always stop abruptly just before it reaches the creek bed. Many believe this to be the sound of Myrtle as she plummets to the ground. Myrtle is also seen walking around below the area where her broken body was found as if looking for something. It is believed that she is eternally looking for the child she lost, unaware that her baby survived and lived a full life. Myrtle is a woman who drove herself and her three-year-old daughter to the Suicide Bridge, threw her child over the railing and then jumped herself. The child survived after falling into a tall pepper tree; however, her mother was so badly injured that she writhed in pain for two hours before dying from her injuries. Myrtle's daughter once said that it was only by angelic intervention that she did not die when her mother tossed her from the bridge.

There have been numerous reports of a gruff male voice being heard from among the trees and rocks below the bridge. The voice seems to be blaming a woman for something, although no one truly knows what he means when calling out, "It's her fault." It is believed that this spirit may be that of Charles Winkelman. It seems that Charles's wife had been cheating on him, and he'd had enough. He drove with his wife to the Colorado Street Bridge with the idea of killing himself while she watched, but when they arrived at the span, he dragged his wife out of the car with the intent of taking her with him. She managed to fight off her husband, and he then threw himself over the railings. This happened in 1934, and his spirit has

Family members place these locks at the spot where their loved ones decided on a permanent solution to their temporary problem.

been wandering below the bridge ever since. Many poking around below the bridge claim to have heard strange voices that whisper things that can be heard but are always so quiet that the words are impossible to make out. There are other reports about figures that lurk just beyond one's vision within the thick brush that dominates the arroyo. Some of these figures have been reported as shadow men or simply as dark figures and black shadows. No one knows who or what these elusive spirits are or whether they are good, evil or simply neutral in nature.

Over the years, so many folks have come to the bridge to seek a permanent solution to a temporary problem that a suicide prevention system had to be installed to try to keep people from ending their lives. It is said that well over 150 souls died by jumping off the span; 30 deaths have occurred since 2010. The fencing along the bridge does detract from the original beauty of the architecture, but it has seriously slowed the carnage of those seeking to do themselves harm. With the sheer number of deaths associated with the Colorado Street Bridge, it may not come as a surprise that this work of engineering art is a place known by locals and visitors alike as an extremely haunted location.

Suicide is never the answer to a problem. Life is precious, and there is nothing that can't be overcome with time and patience. If any of my readers ever feel so despondent that they think suicide is their only recourse, please talk to someone, get help and stay alive. We are all better off with those we love by our side; don't let depression win. National Suicide Prevention Lifeline: 1-800-273-8255

17

HOLLYWOOD FOREVER CEMETERY

Cemeteries. That one word conjures up visions of tombstones, flowers and sorrow. Not many people who think about cemeteries envision lying on the grass, watching a horror movie, comedy film or classic western. Especially watching these movies surrounded by our favorite movie star, author or other Hollywood dignitary—well, at least their gravestones. But that is exactly what you get at the Hollywood Forever Cemetery in eastern Hollywood and directly along Route 66, now called Santa Monica Boulevard. This cemetery, which abuts the back wall of Paramount Studios, has so many of our matinee idols and movie stars buried here that it would take a couple of full days to see all of their grave markers. The cemetery, in an odd move, shows movies on a big screen projector on the grass among the graves and crypts of the famous. Watching a movie or just going for a visit, one must keep on the lookout for the Hollywood elite, both in the grave and in spirit; for you see, some of our favorite stars are not content to stay in their resting places.

Virginia Rappe was an up-and-coming movie star in the early days of cinema; she had a bright future until she met Roscoe "Fatty" Arbuckle and attended one of his famous bacchanals, where she met her death. Arbuckle was acquitted in a court of law regarding her death, but his career was over by the end of the trial. Virginia, however, was dead. Virginia Rappe was buried at Hollywood Forever Cemetery along the shore of the Sylvan Lake in the Garden of Legends. The peaceful spot along the pristine lake has not allowed Virginia to rest, however. Many people have reported hearing the sounds of screaming coming up from below her gravestone as loud as if the ground wasn't covering her. Others have felt what seems to be heartbeats pulsating underneath their feet. Others, placing their hands on the ground where the beat is felt, feel the rhythm of a heartbeat and can tell that it increases for a moment as they touch the ground before it finally fades away. On rare occasions, people report seeing a young woman, dressed in clothes right out of the 1920s, sitting on the edge of the lake. They say that the woman appears to be crying, and when they try to approach, the woman simply vanishes from sight. It is then they realize the woman is sitting next to Rappe's grave.

When at the cemetery, if you enter the Abbey of the Psalms mausoleum, you will find an ideal spot for a bit of celebrity grave hunting. Here you will find a few stars from the past, including Judy Garland, Victor Fleming, Iron Eyes Cody and Charlie Chaplin, to name just a few. You will also find the crypt of Clifton Webb. Some may know Webb from his films *Three Coins in the Fountain*, *Mr. Belvedere Goes to College* and *Cheaper by the Dozen*. Webb passed away in 1966, but since that time, he has refused to stay in the vault where his body was interred. There have been many reports of people walking the corridor where Webb's crypt is located and hearing whispered voices as they have passed his vault. Reports of unusual cold spots, strange lights and the scent of Webb's signature cologne have come from the Abbey of the Psalms. For those who smell the cologne, the aroma is usually followed by the sight of Webb leaning against his marker. He is always dressed in his finest suit, hat and coat, as Webb, who was always a stickler for looking his best, wouldn't have it any other way in death. Clifton is usually seen with a kind but mischievous look and smile on his face. Webb will stare at his visitors for a few seconds, push back from the wall, tip his hat and slowly walk away from them until he vanishes from sight.

It seems obvious that Mr. Webb has not relinquished his ties to Hollywood or his fans. As he was always known as someone who craved the camera and adored his fans, it is not a stretch to believe that Webb was not ready to give them up even in death. If you decide to visit the Abbey of the Psalms and happen upon Mr. Webb, return the smile and let him know you still appreciate his appearances, even if the camera isn't present.

Perhaps the most famous spirit at Hollywood Forever may also be the most recent. The Cathedral Mausoleum in the southeast corner of the cemetery is where, in 1926, silent film heartthrob Rudolph Valentino was laid to rest. The year after his passing, and for the next thirty years, Ditra Flame came to his mausoleum to leave one red rose. According to Miss Flame, the reason

The Lady in Black still brings Valentino a single red rose on the anniversary of his passing, even after her own death.

for her devotion stemmed from the time when she was fourteen years old, and deathly ill. As a favor to her mother, Valentino would go to the hospital with a single red rose, and place it in her hand. He would sit by her bed to comfort her, and once told her, "You're not going to die at all. You are going to live for many more years. One thing for sure, if I die before you do, please come and stay by me because I don't want to be alone." Six years later Rudolph Valentino passed away of complications from surgery to fix an ulcer and appendicitis. Miss Flame never forgot his kindness, or her promise.

Every year, Miss Flame, always dressed in a black mourning dress, made the pilgrimage to place a rose on this kind man's grave. However, as Valentino's fame grew into the 1950s, so did the story of the "Lady in Black," who left a rose, and became an urban legend. Dozens of women, also dressed in black, began to copy Miss Flame, and would come to his grave every year with roses. So many so, that Flame stopped showing up altogether. More and more women began showing up every year, and this has started a growing disagreement on who the original Lady in Black, might be. There are those who say that Pola Negri, who was said to be Valentino's fiancée, was the mysterious woman; however, we now know that Valentino was gay, and it is hard to believe a beard, or cover wife, would show such devotion. Over

Virginia Rappe's heart is said to still beat and can be felt if you place your hand on her grave.

the years, many women have come forward claiming to be the mysterious Lady in Black, most too young to fit the profile, and the rest not having a believable story. Miss Flame however, seems to have a rock-solid basis in fact with her claims.

Ditra Flame passed away on February 23, 1984, at the age of seventy-eight. Since that year, sightings of a spectral Lady in Black have been reported every year on the anniversary of Valentino's passing. The stories are always the same. A woman dressed in the same mourning gown as the one Miss Flame wore will walk up to the crypt, place a single red rose in the vase, gaze kindly at the marker before placing a kiss on her fingers that she transfers to the stone and then will slowly walk away, fading from view. As the Lady in Black fades, so does the rose until there is no sign that either had been there. It would seem that even in death Miss Flame keeps her promise to make sure Rudolph Valentino will never be alone.

The back wall of Hollywood Forever Cemetery is directly behind, and adjacent to Paramount Studios. Paramount was actually built on cemetery property, and this could be the reason that Paramount is said to be the most haunted movie studio in Hollywood. Whether that is due to the studio being behind the cemetery or the spirits of Hollywood's past still longing for the lights and action of the cameras, Hollywood Forever Cemetery is one place that those looking for ghosts should not miss. While you are there, maybe take in an old flick and get into the spirit of the movie by watching it with one of the stars in the film.

18

THE LOS ANGELES ARBORETUM

Anyone who remembers the original *Fantasy Island* television show has seen the Los Angeles Arboretum or at least a small part of it. When Tattoo, played by Hervé Villechaize, rings the bell and calls out, "The plane, boss, the plane," the actor does so from the tower of the Queen Anne Cottage that stands within this botanical garden in the city of Arcadia. This beautiful urban paradise is filled with flowers for everyone's taste, trees that produce shade to keep you cool in the summer and dry during those sudden winter storms along with walkways where your mind can wander in peace and tranquility as it takes in a sylvan atmosphere that soothes the very soul. The Los Angeles Arboretum has it all, including a few ghosts to keep one company while strolling the grounds.

Once part of the Rancho Santa Anita land grant, the first owner was Hugo Reid, a Scotsman who built an adobe in 1840 for himself and his Native American wife that can still be seen today. After Reid tired of ranching, the property went through a series of owners until 1875, when Elias "Lucky" Baldwin purchased the rancho. Baldwin made substantial improvements both on the land and around the lakes of his property, and many in the area had high hopes that he would truly allow it to become the "fairy spot of the valley" that many had once called it. The Queen Anne Cottage that we see today, and on *Fantasy Island* reruns, was built by Baldwin in 1885 on a peninsula that juts out into the lake for his family home. When Baldwin died from pneumonia in 1909, his daughter Anita moved to a home she'd had constructed and leased the Queen Anne to Chief Buffalo Child Long Lance, after the death of her stepmother.

Long Lance was an Indian activist, actor and author. As an author, Long Lance devoted his writings to tribal legends and traditions and was a well-known critic toward the government's treatment of the Native Americans. His books and his activism, along with others' belief in his Cherokee heritage, garnered him fame, money and prestige, all the things that Long Lance had craved from childhood. With notoriety came offers; one of these was to appear in a film, which Long Lance gladly accepted. It was this film, however, that led to his downfall. The movie, titled *The Silent Enemy*, was to depict Native people as they really were, not what people wanted them to be; as such, the film employed quite a few Native actors. One of these began to question Long Lance's heritage, and with Long Lance being unable to give a proper lineage, the truth finally came out that Chief Buffalo Child Long Lance had been lying for years.

Long Lance was in fact an African American named Sylvester Clark Long, born to formerly enslaved parents; wanting to remove himself from his heritage, he adopted that of a Cherokee chief. Once the truth was revealed, Long was ruined, and in 1932, Long put a gun to his head and pulled the trigger. Sylvester Long's body was found inside the now famous Queen Anne Cottage.

Chief Long Lance may have ended his life at the Arboretum, but he apparently decided not to leave this beautiful home. Over the years since his death, even with the property turned into the arboretum and officially opened in 1955, many reports of Long making himself known have come from the old Queen Anne Cottage. Almost from the day Long took his life, folks began hearing sounds of low moans coming from the house. The strange thing is, many of these moans sound as if they are coming from a female. There are those who believe these may be coming from one of Baldwin's many wives, one of whom is thought to have passed away in the Queen Anne Cottage. Other moans that have been heard are obviously those of a male in deep distress. Could it be the drunken last regrets of Long, just before the bullet goes through his brain?

Since the Queen Anne has been open for tours, there have been many reports from people who have seen what they describe as "a Native American man" walking in the hallway. On other occasions, he is seen simply as a "dark gentleman in fine clothes from the 1920s." It isn't just the tourists who have seen Mr. Long in the Queen Anne Cottage. During the filming of the show *Fantasy Island*, quite a few people in the cast and crew have not only seen Chief Buffalo Child Long Lance but also claimed to have spoken to him. It would seem that Mr. Long likes to give advice and encouragement to those in the industry he was set to begin a new career in before it all came crashing down. Nice to know that even in his despair, his kindness toward others has remained. It is said that Long Lance also made an appearance in the TV show as one of the crowd extras.

Chief Buffalo Child Long Lance is not the only spirit seen inside the Queen Anne Cottage. Many folks have seen a man staring at them from the windows at night while the house is shut and locked up tight. A few who have seen pictures of the bearded Baldwin claim that there is no mistaking that it is he who was looking at them. "Lucky" Baldwin has also been seen sitting in areas of the Queen Anne as if it is just another day in his life and as though he hadn't a care in the world. The love the man had for his home was well known, so it isn't a stretch to believe that he would return if he was still on the earthly plane. Other reports that have come from the Queen Anne Cottage include sounds of whispered voices being heard while passing an otherwise empty room, having a heavy feeling suddenly come over the unwary and the sensation of being watched everywhere one goes while touring the home.

The Queen Anne Cottage is not the only place at the arboretum where spirits have been seen. Many folks strolling the pristine walkways have reported catching glimpses of both male and female apparitions ambling along either in front of them, behind them, even on a few occasions on adjacent sidewalks. They say that these spirits will stroll along and then slowly fade from sight. Most but not all of these reports come from those out at the arboretum in the evening hours. These ghosts are not relegated to one area but have been seen all over the complex.

The Los Angeles Arboretum has become a star in its own right, with its many appearances on *Fantasy Island*; the arboretum has appeared in many other TV shows and movies. From quite a few *Tarzan* films to the movies *Anaconda* and *Jurassic Park*, there are few who have not seen the arboretum with their own eyes. What many have not witnessed are the many spirits who call the arboretum home. As such, this is another one of those places that any good ParaTraveler would not want to miss.

19

THE AZTEC HOTEL

In the city of Monrovia, California, directly along one of the old alignments of Route 66, lies one of the only Mayan Revival buildings left in existence: the Aztec Hotel. At one time, the Aztec Hotel was a main watering hole for Hollywood's elite, bootleggers and mob bosses. Once the Mother Road was realigned, the Aztec fell to the dregs of society to become a house of ill repute, drugs and gangs. However, the future again looks bright for this wonderfully kitschy old hotel. Monrovia has cleaned up the drugs and gangs, and the hotel has a new owner who is determined to bring this Route 66 original back to the prominence it deserves. I know that the ghosts residing at the Aztec must be excited, as those who frequent the hotel's Mayan Bar and ghost walk can attest.

In a March 2001 article, the *Los Angeles Times* wrote, "For architectural historians, the Aztec is a gem listed on the National Register of Historic Places. But its other fans include psychics and mediums who are enthralled by a hotel where some guests may never have checked out." One of the spirits at the Aztec is said to be a ghost that goes by the name Razzle Dazzle. This supposed Kansas-born soiled dove is said to wear her dark hair in a finger-wave style and carry a long cigarette holder. Both of these were popular in the 1920s, leading many to believe that this young woman died during that period. It is thought that Razzle Dazzle died after taking a customer to her room and that he either didn't want to pay or quibbled over her price. During a struggle, Razzle was shoved down, hitting her head on the radiator, which killed her. Many who have stayed in room 120 would wake up and see Ms. Dazzle standing at the foot of their bed or feel

The historic Aztec Hotel is the only example of Mayan Revival architecture remaining in the country.

her lying down next to them. This story has a few different tellings, but the ghost stories remain the same.

In the lobby of the hotel and just opposite the front desk is a women's restroom. Reports have come from this bathroom of doors swinging open as ladies were using the stall even though the door was securely latched. Disembodied voices have been reported, with some claiming to have their names called out as they were freshening up in front of the mirror and in a few rare cases seeing a deathly pale face. The apparition seems to be peering over their shoulder, but when the guest turns to look, no one is there. Those touring the hotel catch glimpses of wispy shadows in the hallways, around the lobby and even on the patio. These figures are visible for a second and then gone as quickly as they appeared. It is believed that many of these figures may be the spirits of the women who worked at the brothel.

While doing research for this book, I had the pleasure of meeting Willie, the manager of the hotel's Mayan Bar and Grill. Willie was gracious enough to give my friend Louis Montero and me a tour of the Aztec Hotel and regaled us with a few of the ghostly happenings that he had witnessed in the years working for the bar and helping restore the hotel. Willie said that in the first six months he worked here, many things happened that made him question remaining employed at the hotel. Willie said that just after he hired

Left: This doorway leading into the VIP room is where manager Willie Flores saw a spirit sitting in a chair as if waiting for someone.

Below: Up this stairway lie the guest rooms for the hotel. It is said that many of the rooms are haunted.

on at the Mayan Bar, he was walking through the VIP room and began hearing whistles. He said that after looking around and finding no one, he continued on his way and didn't think much about it. Later, he heard the same whistles as he was walking through on the return trip. Then, when the same thing happened a few more times, he realized that it could not be a coincidence. When he heard the whistle close to his ear, he demanded that whoever was doing it stop, and he never heard the whistles again—but his coworkers did. Another phenomenon that Willie told us about was when he was in the lobby and noticed a man sit down in a chair placed between the VIP room and the hotel lobby by one of the staff. Willie said the man had black hair and was wearing black pants and a green shirt. Thinking that the gentleman was waiting for the bar manager, Willie went and told her he was waiting. Confused, both Willie and the manager went back to the lobby, but the man was nowhere to be found. The manager mentioned the hotel ghosts to Willie, and since then, he keeps a tablecloth over the chair in the hopes that he won't see the spirit again.

Willie told us that once, as he was walking through the VIP room, he felt as if someone was watching him. He said his head began to ache, and his legs began to feel heavy. When he was near the center of the room, he felt someone come up behind him and push him; of course, nobody was there, but he knew he had been shoved. Once Willie got back to the bar, he told the bartender not to ask him to go back to the cooler because he would have to refuse the order.

Willie told us that down in the basement, there are a few rooms that once served as a speakeasy for the hotel during Prohibition. He told us that there were at least two tunnels leading away from the Aztec that had been used for the Hollywood stars, politicians and mob bosses to avoid any raiding police. He also said that one of these rooms, the Green Room as it is now called, seems to have a portal or, as some call it, a vortex that allows spirits to come into our realm whenever they so choose. He said that he has never had any sort of paranormal activity in the room but that many visiting psychics, and a few ghost hunters, back when the hotel was allowing investigations, said that the Green Room is the true heart of the hotel's paranormal happenings.

As of this writing, the Aztec Hotel has not yet reopened; however, it is hoped that the renovations will soon be completed. For now, one can still visit this wonderful piece of paranormal California and old Route 66 by coming and enjoying good food, good drink and good company, both living and dead, at the Mayan Bar and Grill. When stopping in, tell them hello from me, the ParaTraveler, and have a hauntingly good time.

20

DISNEYLAND

To all who come to this happy place; welcome! Disneyland is your land. Here, age relives fond memories of the past, and here, youth may savor the challenge, and promise of the future. Disneyland is dedicated to the ideals, the dreams, and the hard facts that have created America, with the hope that it will be a source of joy, and inspiration to all the world.

With these words, Walt Disney opened what would become the world's premier amusement park. But this wonderland in Anaheim, California, is much more than just an amusement park. For hundreds of thousands of folks around the world, Disney theme parks have become a way of life. For these fans of Disney, while not at the park itself, they anxiously await the next big Disney movie, or they may be found at the nearest Disney store or at one of the theme parks Disney Walk areas outside of the park shopping and dining to be near the place they have come to love so much. A way of life? For many, their love of all things Disney has *become* their life.

Walt Disney had a dream of a place where families could come together, enjoy each other's company and relax. A place where they could forget their worries for just awhile, dream of a simpler life and explore their fantasies in a safe and nurturing place. At the time Disneyland was created, amusement parks were anything but family oriented. Most were poorly kept up, filled with teens snogging on the benches and the rides, and most drew an element of lawless thugs out looking for trouble. Walt knew that a place was needed

Once you pass this sign above the entrance to Disneyland, you have truly entered a fun new world of adventure…in more ways than one. *Courtesy of Louis Montero.*

that would change all that. The idea came to him one day while watching his kids play during a family outing in Griffith Park in Los Angeles. He smiled as he thought about how happy his kids would be in a place such as the one he envisioned. Many folks were writing to him to ask for tours of his now famous Disney Studios, so Walt decided right then and there that it was time he realized their dream and his.

When Disneyland first opened on July 17, 1955, things didn't go exactly as planned. Walt, never daunted, made the best of it. The opening was a live televised event on ABC, and those in attendance were treated to guests such as Ronald Reagan, Art Linkletter and Debbie Reynolds. Even with some things going awry, folks were in awe of what Disney had accomplished. With eighteen rides spread over five "lands," along with a Main Street, a castle and other wonders, Disneyland was sure to become a hit. Over the years, Disneyland grew: more rides and attractions were added; others were removed to make way for grander and more modern rides. Rollercoasters, water flumes and any other attraction one could possibly dream of could all be found at Mickey Mouse's home.

Today, Disneyland has been joined by its sister Disney's California Adventures theme park, and one can go back and forth to each park on a single day's visit. There are now six Disney resort locations around the world, including Paris, Hong Kong, Japan and Shanghai, and more parks than one can count here in the United States, with Disney World topping them all with four main parks: Magic Kingdom, Animal Kingdom, Epcot Center and Hollywood Studios. But as spectacular and popular as they all are, none comes close to the love Disney fans feel toward the original House of Mickey or the dedication they have to this, the first theme park in the world. So loved is Disneyland that it is no surprise that many want to spend their eternity in the "Happiest Place on Earth."

Disney, even though the corporation doesn't like talking about the spirits that haunt the park, can in all honesty no longer deny their existence. One can understand corporate's hesitancy, as they want to put forth the image of happiness and life; however, if one thinks about the fact that these spirits have returned to Disneyland for just that reason, it should make them feel happy they are providing an eternity of joy to those who remain in the Magic Kingdom. Disney has always had the safety of their guests at the front of their agenda; this has always been reflected in their constant vigilance in and around the parks. Even with this attentiveness to guests, Disney cannot control people's disregard for their own safety or that of others who are near them. Because of this, unfortunate things can and will occur. I will not dwell on this, as Disney cannot be held responsible.

One of the most prolific tales of spirits at Disneyland comes from the aptly named Haunted Mansion ride. Legend has it the spirit of a young boy is often seen in various areas of the ride; this child has been seen trying to catch the ghosts that fly around the table and dance in the banquet hall. He has also been seen hiding behind gravestones in the cemetery section of the ride and peeking at guests as they pass by in their "Doom Buggy." It would seem that this child is certainly enjoying himself in what was perhaps his favorite ride at the park. This child has, on occasion, been spotted at the exit from the ride quietly sobbing. It is believed that he may be looking for his mother and wondering why she left him. It turns out that the mother, without permission from the park, sprinkled the boy's ashes within the Haunted Mansion. It has become obvious to most that this boy spends most of his time having fun rather than fretting about his mother.

The spreading of ashes around Disneyland has become such a problem for the parks that Disney now has staff who walk the rides after the park closes looking for telltale signs that folks have left their loved ones behind, and there are cameras in most if not all the attractions watching for this activity. Disney and cast members do their best to dissuade guests from this

The Matterhorn is perhaps the most recognized icon of Disneyland after the immortal Mickey Mouse. *Courtesy of Louis Montero.*

behavior but still find this happening on many occasions. There seems to be nowhere at the parks where folks don't want their deceased loved one to spend eternity.

Many guests have written about the activity they have seen, such as this submission to hauntedoc.com by Jacqueline S:

> *Once my mom and I endeavored to ride by ourselves the Haunted Mansion [ride] on the last ride of the night. We got in [line] just as they closed the gates at midnight and waited a minute in the gallery to let the other guests board first. Once some space had passed, we got in our doom buggy for our solo midnight ride. But as we rounded Madam Leota's room, we were shocked and disappointed. We looked across the room and saw full doom buggies! Men, women and children. We figured they opened up the gates to let one more large group on. Oh well. When we got to the end to disembark, there were no cast members present so we decided to linger in the mausoleum before ascending to the world of the living. And what did we see? Nothing but empty doom buggies! No people at all! We waited and waited. No one was there. True story.*

One of the most well-known and most ridden rides at any Disney Park, the Haunted Mansion at Disneyland may in fact be as its name implies. *Courtesy of Louis Montero.*

There is another ride where folks have placed their loved ones for everlasting fun. I am talking about the Pirates of the Caribbean attraction. Many folks who have ridden this water ride have claimed to see a small boy sitting in one of the empty boats or even in an empty row of seats in an otherwise full boat. The child rarely responds to the ride's thrills or to anyone trying to communicate with him. The boy just stares straight ahead, doesn't bother anyone and simply vanishes just before the boat comes to the top of the hill where the ride ends. After the boat he was riding in comes around to where guests exit and then enter for the next go round, he again appears once more to take in the fun of this groundbreaking attraction. The following story, also posted on hauntedoc.com, comes from Adee R.:

Pirates of the Caribbean's ride. We sat on the last row of the boat so no one was behind us. I sat on the left side of the boat. Right when we are approaching the big battle of the ships, I got bumped on the side of my head. No one was behind me and it came from behind. I wasn't in the middle, so it wasn't the people sitting next to me that bumped me. I was recording on my phone and upon review, I noticed a…shadow come in to view for just a few seconds when I got bumped on my head.

Just above the entrance to the Pirates of the Caribbean ride is where Walt Disney once had a room where he would entertain his guests; this became the Walt Disney Gallery. Here, guests of Disneyland could walk through and see marvelous works of art depicting the many scenes that can be found in the park, as well as those that no longer exist but have been replaced by newer and bigger attractions. There have been many reports from people touring the gallery who have seen Walt gazing at folks walking through. All of those who have seen him have said that he sports a smile and looks as if he is happy that people are enjoying themselves. Many have said that just seeing him and knowing he is happy brings a smile to their faces as well.

The Walt Disney Gallery is not the only place where Walt has been seen. The wishing well, near Sleeping Beauty's Castle, was a favorite spot for Mr. Disney to sit and relax while enjoying the happiness that he was seeing in his guests. Even today, guests and cast members have said they have seen Walt sitting nearby or standing next to the wishing well just watching people passing by and smiling as he did when he was alive. Walt also had an office above the firehouse near the beginning of Main Street. A cast member said that one night while she was in this very office she felt a presence behind her; when she turned, there was no there, but she still felt as if someone was present. She said that she wasn't scared or alarmed and that she felt that whoever was with her meant her no harm. The cast member went on to say that as she was leaving, she heard a low whisper come from just behind her: "I'm still here." Many believe that it was Walt letting her know that he still watches over his beloved park.

There are many other areas within Disneyland that are known to have paranormal occurrences. The Matterhorn and Space Mountain, Tom Sawyer Island and New Orleans Square, even the It's a Small World ride is said to have children and adults both still enjoying the happy theme and wonderful music of this famous attraction. My apologies, the song will be out of your mind in a few hours. The haunts at Disneyland are less than frightening, and the spirits that have remained are anything but lost souls. With the fun and fantasy that Disney provides its guests, it is a wonder anyone could think that a spirit that has come back to the park or the Disneyland Hotel would have done it for any other reason than to have an afterlife filled with fun, fantasy and Mickey Mouse.

Walt has been seen happily walking down Main Street and in other areas of the park, and one can only imagine what the man who brought so many millions of people happiness must think about what his creation has become—and what the future may still hold. We should all give thanks to

The Disney Gallery on Main Street USA is said to be haunted by none other than Walt Disney. *Courtesy of Louis Montero*.

Mr. Disney for this creation and place of joy. So, when visiting Disneyland or California Adventures, staying at one of the marvelous hotels or simply shopping at Downtown Disney, if you happen to see one of the happy haunts, just say hi and give them a smile, because I'm sure they will be smiling at you. And remember, there is always room for one more.

21

THE BANNING HOUSE

Phineas Banning may have had more to do with the creation of modern-day Wilmington, San Pedro and the entire Los Angeles Harbor area than any other person. Originally from Wilmington, Delaware, Banning came to San Pedro, California, in 1851, and immediately knew he would make this place his home. Taking employment at the small pier owned by Spanish Don Sepulveda and his family, he soon began driving the Sepulvedas' wagons up to the pueblo of Los Angeles and across the western desert to market the family's goods. It took a while, but Banning finally made enough money to buy a wagon of his own.

By 1853, Banning, with the help of investor Harris Newmark, was able to open up a wagon route to Salt Lake City, selling to the Mormon outpost there. This trade route, along with others he had acquired, allowed Banning to amass a good deal of money. With the money he had earned, Banning bought 640 acres of land near the harbor and started his own town, which he named Wilmington in honor of his hometown. Seeing the potential of the natural harbor, Banning began to build it up, first by digging a canal to his growing town, which allowed heavy freight to be shipped there. He also erected docks and finally petitioned the U.S. government to certify the Port of San Pedro as an international harbor. For all of his hard work, the folks living in the area bestowed the honorary title of port admiral on Phineas Banning. He would henceforth all but demand people refer to him as Admiral Banning. Banning went on to construct his own railroad to get goods from the port to the city of Los Angeles, built his own telegraph and all but single-handedly created what is now one of the busiest ports in the country—all while amassing a fortune for himself and his family.

Banning built a marvelous Greek Revival home for himself and his family, and it became a centerpiece for the entire community. The Bannings held elaborate parties they called "regales," where senators, business leaders, army generals, sea captains and foreign ambassadors came to not only join in the festivities but also conduct trade. On occasion, the Bannings hosted parties for the townsfolk to let them know they were not forgotten or ignored. Banning developed a stellar reputation with both the common folk and the gentry.

When the American Civil War broke out, Banning, being a staunch Unionist, approached the Federal government and offered them a large parcel of his land adjacent to his home to be used as an army post. This would become one of the best-equipped and most sought-after posts for Union soldiers during the war. Banning owned a fair amount of land on Santa Catalina Island, and he allowed the Union navy to use his ports and facilities there. For all of his efforts, the United States of America granted Banning the honorary title of general. Banning used both designations when introducing himself, but much preferred admiral over general.

Phineas Banning died in a hotel room in the city of San Francisco from injuries suffered when a wagon knocked him down in 1884. The Banning family continued to live in the Greek Revival mansion until 1925, when the City of Los Angeles purchased the home to turn it into a museum. The Drum Barracks, as the Civil War post had been named, was later turned into a museum as well, and Banning's holdings on Catalina Island were sold to private investors. The home the Bannings had in Two Harbors has become one of the only hotels on that section of the island and is the only upscale inn there. It would seem, however, that Phineas Banning was not ready to leave his home—even in death.

Over the years, many people have claimed to see Banning walking around the grounds of his property; he has been spotted in the garden, the barn and various other locations he was known to enjoy in life. The barn at the museum now holds a variety of wagons, carts and carriages, and when glimpsed, Banning seems to be making sure that his conveyances are in good working order. The descriptions of Banning are always the same: a gentleman wearing Victorian-era finery of suit and tie. He walks with the air of a man of distinction, but his bearing is always one of kindness. He will sometimes turn and look at those watching him, give a brief smile and vanish from view. Banning has also been seen inside his mansion. He

The Banning House museum was the site of Phineas Banning's galas, and Banning himself may still be in the mansion enjoying his parties.

is often seen sitting in one of the chairs in what was the smoking room, as if he is entertaining guests; the smell of cigar smoke often accompanies these sightings.

The parlor of the house is where the ladies would retire to talk among themselves while the men smoked, drank and told their tall tales; here perfume can often be smelled. Six Banning children passed away in the home, and there have been numerous reports of children's laughter coming from the second floor, where the nursery and kid's bedrooms would have been. Many people believe that the children they hear laughing and playing are the Banning children who died in the house. The third floor of the mansion is also said to be haunted by children, but these are believed to be the kids of the servants who lived there. The sound of children laughing and playing can also be heard on the grounds near where the old schoolhouse used to be. Also heard on the grounds of the museum are sounds of phantom horses that seem as if they are pulling carriages or wagons; these are actually heard by those living near the museum, and on rare occasions residents have claimed to have seen spectral images.

The Banning Museum represents a time in California history when the state was still in its infancy with all of the growing pains and strife that come with growing up. Maybe that is why the Banning House and the nearby Drum Barracks Museum (the army post that Banning donated during the Civil War) are so haunted. Whatever the case may be, a trip to either of these wonderfully haunted locations is a must for those seeking the paranormal.

22

WARNER GRAND THEATER

The Warner Grand Theater was built at a time when going to the movies was as much a social event as it was an entertainment. It was a time when women wore their finest gowns and jewelry, and men would don suit and tie, along with their favorite hat, for nothing more than a movie and a chance to be seen with their best gal for a night out on the town at the local movie palace. The term *movie palace* may sound strange to our modern ears, but it was apt for many of the theaters that were showing films with Charlie Chaplin, Thelma Todd, Buster Keaton and Clara Bow. To the fans, movies were more than just a show; they were an escape from the trying times of the Depression, a way to live their fantasies, if only for a short time, and to dream of better times. Those making the movies knew this and built theaters to rival the palaces of Europe, and the cinemas that did it best were the Warner theaters in and around Hollywood.

The Warner Grand Theater in San Pedro, California, was but one of three grand movie palaces built by Warner Bros. and unfortunately is the only one still in existence today. The buildings the other theaters occupied are still there, but one is a collection of cheap shops, and the other, still on Hollywood Boulevard, is part of a telephone company and houses equipment. Neither resembles what they once were, and with today's need for speedy build up and cheap materials, we will never see their like again. Even the Warner Grand was almost lost, but thankfully the Grand Vision Foundation had the foresight to save this historic theater for future generations.

When the Warner Grand Theater opened on January 20, 1931, Jack Warner stood in front of the closed doors, cleared his voice and loudly spoke to the gathered crowd: "Here I give you the castle of your dreams." He then opened the doors. Theater patrons were shown in by white-gloved ushers, and once inside, they found concession stands selling every sort of sweets, treats and sugary delights as well as candy girls wandering the aisles selling the things that may have been forgotten or seconds of items already eaten. Restroom attendants were on hand with towels, cologne and other sundries for the men and soaps, towels and lotions for the ladies. On stage before the movie was shown acts ranging from magicians to clowns that would keep the audience amused, and when the lights went down on this first night, Warner Studios premiered the movie *Going Wild*.

The Warner Grand would go on to become one of the most visited theaters in the Los Angeles area because of the opulent Art Deco décor, the wonderful Warner Bros. movies it showed and the sheer grandeur of the theater itself. Unfortunately, when the U.S. government broke up the monopolies that the studios held over independent theaters, forcing them to show only certain studios' films, along with the advent of television, the fortunes of the Warner Grand fell precipitously. When, in the 1980s, video rentals came on the scene, the theater could not survive and was sold. The

The mundane appearance of the building belies the opulence one will find inside this movie palace.

theater was reinvented as Teatro Juarez; had its Art Deco removed to be replaced by gaudy green, gold and red throughout; and began showing only Spanish-language films. This iteration lasted a few years, and afterward, the Warner Grand sat empty heading for the wrecking ball.

Today, the Warner Grand Theater, saved by the dedicated folks of the Grand Vision Foundation, have brought back the name, the movies, the Art Deco and the allure for which the Warner Grand had always been known. One thing that the foundation didn't need to bring back, something that had always been there—through the hard times, the Spanish iteration and even the vacancy when all was thought lost—were the spirits that call the Warner Grand home.

Tales of ghostly goings-on started well before the theater's closure after Teatro Juarez shut down. Since the early 1960s, people shopping at night, along with those working late in the shops and stores along Sixth Street, would see people gathered in front of the Warner Grand just milling about as if waiting for a show to start. This may not seem strange being in front of a movie house, but these patrons would be gathered at times the theater was closed for the evening and even sometimes during the day when there was no matinee scheduled. Over the years, these tales of ghostly moviegoers have not diminished but grown. Many witnesses have reported seeing these specters milling about and, on occasion, entering the theater, passing through closed doors as if to see their favorite film. One element that has been reported quite often is that these ghostly theater patrons are all dressed as if from different eras in the Warner Grand's history. Some are dressed in the finery that was common in the early days, others in clothing reminiscent of the '40s and '50s, and still others look like they could be from the '60s and '70s. It seems that no matter what era the Warner Grand was in existence, the theater had many devoted fans.

It would seem, given that the Warner Grand San Pedro was Jack Warner's favorite, that the man himself still comes to watch the movies and shows the theater plays today. Many people have asked about the gentleman wearing the "fine suit and tie from the 1930s" seen in the back of the balcony. They want to know if he is a reenactor hired to add realism to the Art Deco movie palace. Those who have been shown pictures of the Warner brothers always point to Jack as the man they saw in the theater. Others have been startled by Jack when they see him flash a warm smile, nod his head and then vanish before their eyes as the lights come up after the movie has ended. It was well known that Jack Warner would come to the theater to relax, watch the movies and enjoy the solitude he needed after a long week at the studio.

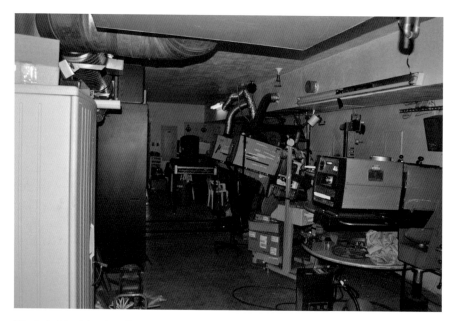

The helpful spirit who still works in the projection booth at the Warner Grand has earned the respect and thanks of the living projectionists.

He would always sit in the back of the balcony, in the same seat where the specter has been seen sitting.

Another spirit seen often at the Warner Grand is that of what can only be described as a dedicated employee. The man was one of the projectionists at the movie palace and by his clothing, it was sometime in the late 1940s or early 1950s. The man has been seen rewinding and loading ghostly film into the projectors, and while movies are playing, the living projectionists have seen the man watching the equipment intently, making sure nothing is going amiss. There have even been times when a projectionist has gone to the restroom or otherwise been away from the projection room when something is going wrong, only to find the problem fixed by the time they get back to the room to fix it themselves. This helpful employee of yore has even been seen working on the projector just as a film is about to jam or slip from the reel, saving the audience from a wait or skip in the movie. No one knows the name of this old projectionist, and none of those working the projection room today find his presence unnerving; on the contrary, most everyone at the Warner Grand is grateful he is there to help.

Other spectral goings-on include the scents of women's perfume and men's cologne wafting from empty rooms, the sounds of whispered conversation emanating from nowhere and the overwhelming aroma of grease-based make-up even when no show is scheduled and stage shows have been absent from the theater for months. Voices and music have been heard coming from the empty orchestra pit, cold spots and EVP are common and even the bathroom area has been known to have reports of activity.

The Warner Grand Theater is one of those places that every theater aficionado must see. Its Art Deco grandeur, its early Americana charm and the sheer beauty of the theater itself harken back to a time when life seemed slower, the country seemed newer and the future seemed brighter than one could imagine. When coming to the Warner Grand, get ready for a wonderful movie with other film fans, and keep in mind that the person setting next to you may be much older than you think. They might have stopped aging decades before coming to the Warner Grand to enjoy the show with you.

23

RMS *QUEEN MARY*

No book about the haunts of Southern California would be complete without the most venerable ship ever to sail the seas. The *Queen Mary* is docked in Long Beach, California, and at the time of this writing is in peril of being scrapped. This would be a sad end to one of the grandest and most historically important ships in the world.

Launched in September 1936, the *Queen Mary* was at that time the pinnacle of shipbuilding and would go on to set records that even today are still unbroken. It set the all-time passenger capacity record during World War II with over sixteen thousand, held the speed record for crossing the Atlantic numerous times and drove Hitler crazy by being so fast that no submarine or ship could sink it. After the war, the *Queen Mary* and its sister ship *Queen Elizabeth* ruled the Atlantic passenger trade, with the *Queen Mary* carrying royalty, movie stars, dignitaries and the extremely wealthy in luxury once unheard of. Surviving a depression and the most destructive war in history, the "Stateliest Ship Afloat" could not survive the growing need to "get there faster, cheaper and with less amenities" that air travel afforded, and the *Queen Mary* was retired. The City of Long Beach purchased the grand ocean liner and converted it into a hotel and tourist attraction on an out-of-the-way spit of land, where it has been docked ever since.

Once the *Queen Mary* opened up after conversion, guests and employees alike began to notice strange things happening aboard the ship, now classified as a building so as to take the responsibility away from the Coast Guard. It began when workers were installing new carpet in some of the lower decks that had still to be opened when they would hear what sounded to them like

Door 13 in shaft alley is where an eighteen-year-old former crewman was crushed while playing chicken with the watertight door. His spirit is still there today and truly likes the ladies.

parties being held in empty banquet rooms and other areas nearby. There were reports that were coming in of seeing men in old Cunard uniforms that hadn't been worn since the '30s and '40s, along with one of the former captains spotted staring at the propeller and huge hole in the side of the ship's hull.

Overnight guests would hear their room's showers or sinks being used even though there was nobody in the bathroom. Other guests would report waking up in the middle of the night with someone staring down at them with a perplexed look on their faces, and some would hear the sound of children's laughter and the cries of a baby coming from the now empty and locked third-class nursery.

Those touring the engine room would see the spectral figure of a young eighteen-year-old crewman who had been crushed by the watertight door, while ladies would feel their hair being touched and the light touch of a hand brush their cheek. Many times, guests reported seeing a woman wearing a white evening gown dancing alone in the old first-class lounge, now the Queen's Salon, and others saw who they believed to be Senior Second Officer Stark, a ship's officer who died after drinking poison he thought was gin, wandering the decks in search of help.

The first-class pool is said to be where a portal between the veil exists and where little Jackie Tourin likes to play.

Perhaps the most beloved and well-known ghost aboard the ship may be the spirit of little Jackie Tourin. No one is sure who this six-year-old child actually is, but she is vocal, precocious and sweet. Little Jackie drowned in the now removed second-class pool. It is believed that she was part of the Bride and Baby Cruises that took place after World War II and that Jackie was traveling under her biological father's name, while her mother was traveling under her new war bride married name. After exhaustive research of records from Cunard, Ellis Island and all other immigration records I could get my hands on, this author came up with the theory as the only logical explanation for why we cannot find this girl's name on any ship records. As the *Queen Mary* tour department is now using this theory as its own, it would seem they agree with me.

The *Queen Mary* shall remain one of the most historic ships that you can still sail on without leaving port. After such a long closure during the pandemic, the spirits onboard may be as anxious to greet visitors and guests as we are to greet them.

24

SAN JUAN CAPISTRANO

The city of San Juan Capistrano is perhaps best known as the place where the swallows return every March to mate and nest at the mission for which the original town was named. What most people may not be aware of is that it has been called and might possibly *be* the most haunted city in all of California. From the mission itself to the Los Rios District, a famous restaurant and even a cemetery just steps off of the busy I-5 freeway, San Juan Capistrano has so many spirits wandering its streets and shops that one would be hard-pressed not to find a ghost if looking for one.

The Mission San Juan Capistrano is notorious for having at least three spirits that make themselves known, and fairly often. Perhaps the most frightening of these is that of a supposedly headless soldier wandering the mission grounds. There is some discrepancy regarding this ghost, as a few reports of his sighting have not mentioned his lack of a cranium. Be that as it may, this Spanish soldier has been seen quite often going about his guard duties and is mainly heedless of the living that wander in his domain. There are a few instances of him taking notice of mission visitors, which seems to indicate this spirit may not in fact be a residual haunting but rather an intelligent apparition, decapitation aside.

Another of the more chilling apparitions that has been witnessed at the mission is the Faceless Monk. This spirit may or may not actually be faceless; however, he garnered this moniker because no one has ever actually seen his face. When this spirit has been seen, it has always been with his back

Above: It is said that a headless Spanish soldier still walks his post at San Juan Capistrano Mission.

Left: A faceless monk is seen strolling down the corridors like this one in the north wing of the mission.

to the onlooker. The apparition is always witnessed in black monk's robes with the cowl pulled up over his head, which is most often bowed down as if in prayer. No one, to this date, has ever claimed to see him from the front. This spirit will only be in view a short time, strolling along the north wing walkways before vanishing from the witness's sight.

The next tale was originally told by a Father O'Sullivan and is less a ghost tale and more of an omen that should have been heeded. The tale tells of a woman by the name of Matilda who lived near the mission and would help clean the church and do the laundry. One day she was spotted looking through the windows during Mass but never entered the church. The padre, who had seen her looking in, went to her and asked why she had failed to come in. Matilda was a bit confused and told the padre that she had not left her house that day and had been nowhere near the mission. The next Sunday, the padre, along with two women and Matilda's brother-in-law, who was working outside the church, again saw her looking in the window during Mass. This time, her brother-in-law went to her to ask why she hadn't gone in to Mass, and again Matilda said she hadn't left the house all day. A few days after this last incidence, Matilda passed away. Many believe that what the padre, the two women and her brother-in-law had witnessed was in fact not Matilda at all but her spirit walking around before death as a sure sign of her impending doom and to allow her loved ones to prepare for her demise. It is said that on rare occasions, Matilda can still be seen at what is left of the old mission.

The most well known of all of the spirits at the mission is also the saddest of all. Magdalena was a beautiful sixteen-year-old who had fallen in love with a simple painter; her father, a man of means, had forbidden her to ever see the man again and swore that she would marry a man of her own social class. Magdalena's father punished his daughter for this forbidden love by forcing Magdalena to confess her sin of love in front of the entire congregation while holding a "penitent candle." The day chosen was December 8, 1812. Magdalena prepared herself, lit the candle and proceeded down the center aisle of the church. As the parishioners watched her, suddenly the church began to shake violently as the 6.9 magnitude Wrightwood/Capistrano Earthquake hit. As the people tried to flee, they found the doors already blocked as the earthquake destroyed the mission, killing Magdalena and the other thirty-nine folks inside. It is said—and has been reported so many times it is hard to dismiss—that Magdalena can still be seen looking through the only window left of the old mission. The building is still here today, and so is Magdalena, grieving her lost love and her life that could have been.

Above: Sixteen-year-old reluctantly penitent bride Magdalena still haunts the old mission where she died, even though the structure is nothing but a shell after collapsing on top of her and other congregants.

Opposite: Avila Modesta's home is now a small café, but Avila, who is thought to have been hanged from the tree in front of her house, still walks the tracks she tried so desperately to have removed.

The mission isn't the only place in San Juan Capistrano that is haunted. The original section of town, known as the Los Rios District, has many spirits wandering the streets and shops that now make up this area. One of the most well known is that of the White Lady of Los Rios. For almost one hundred years, this elegant lady has been spotted under a large pepper tree or strolling down Los Rios Street as if out for a Sunday walk. She was first seen in the 1930s, walking along the railroad tracks that pass in front of Los Rios, leading people to believe that the lady is Modesta Avila. Modesta was an activist who took on the Southern Pacific Railroad, which was trying to take her property. Modesta Avila was convicted in court of "attempted obstruction of a train," sentenced to three years in prison and had her reputation dragged through the mud with lies and other slander. In reality, Avila was most likely convicted because she was Hispanic and a woman. It would seem that today, Modesta Avila may be having the last laugh.

There are other spirits that can be seen wandering around Los Rios Street. Claims of a bruja (witch) by the name of Dona Bernadino being seen in the area are common enough that she has become known as the Phantom of Del Obispo. There is also a young girl spirit that is glimpsed from time to time and appears to be accompanied by a large black dog; this dog is sometimes mistaken as belonging with the bruja, but almost all reports have the dog attached to this little girl.

The Lady of Los Rios is said to still walk the street in front of her house, in the town that she loved.

Other places in the Los Rios with a haunted reputation are the El Adobe Mexican Restaurant, which started out as a private residence and interestingly has an old jail in its basement, along with the Montanez Adobe, the Lupe Combs House, Buford Terrace and Forster Mansion. The cemetery at the mission itself is said to be haunted, but it is the older of two cemeteries. The newer cemetery just off the east side of the I-5 is said to have more ghosts than any other, perhaps in the nation. This cemetery is extremely hard to find without a map and is completely closed to the public with fencing and locks.

As quaint as San Juan Capistrano may be with its wonderful and historic downtown, many restaurants, shops and antiques, what lies underneath the tourist veil is a ParaTravelers' dream of spirits and intrigue that shouldn't be missed.

25

ELFIN FOREST

This once privately owned forest in the Santa Rosa Mountains in rural San Diego County is one of the most beautiful spots in all of California. Its name comes from the former owner's vision of the area and its resemblance to an enchanted forest right out of a J.R.R Tolkien or Terry Brooks fantasy novel. Once you see the Elfin Forest for yourself, you will understand just how apt the name truly is. The forest has become a highly sought-after place for hiking, horseback riding and picnicking with miles of trails and pristine sites spread over the area's approximately seven hundred acres. As magical as the scenery looks, this same Shire-esque atmosphere can also take on an eerie and mysterious feel more akin to that of the evil sorcerer's realm. With its twisted trees, dense foliage and sometimes misty surroundings, it is not hard to imagine strange things peering at you from behind the brush or hidden in the fog. In the Elfin Forest, this may not just be a feeling but an actuality; for you see, these beautiful woods are said to be home to ghosts, witches and mystical occult rituals.

More of an urban legend but with a smattering of truth is the tale of the Questhaven insane asylum. It is said that patients here were routinely tortured and killed and that now these sad individuals haunt the area around the falling foundations of the hospital. There has never been a hospital, let alone an insane asylum here; however, there is the old crumbling foundation of a building that can be found near Questhaven. There are also rumors that there was once a retreat for mental patients here but not the insane. Questhaven has always been a nondenominational religious retreat from the day it was founded by Flower and Lawrence Newhouse.

Strolling through the Elfin Forest is said to be like walking through a J.R.R. Tolkien novel.

Another tale, and one that has a basis in truth, is that of the White Witch. The story goes that a local townswoman and her family were set upon by bandits, and while her husband and son were murdered, she had survived the attack of her would-be killers. As she was being nursed back to health by kindly neighbors, she sought out the local Native American tribe, which taught her the ways of their magic. The woman then went to the "Gypsies"—as they were called at the time—in the area, and they taught her their magic. The woman then combined the two magics and left the village in search of revenge. The woman was never seen again—at least not alive.

Shortly after this lady left her home, folks began telling the tale of a woman in white who was seen along the trails, floating along in silence. She is never seen walking but instead hovering above the ground; on occasion, her feet have vanished and she will be seen as if in a haze or through a smoky vapor. Those who have seen the White Witch never feel threatened or alarmed but give her a wide berth just to be safe.

It is said that the White Witch is often seen along the roadways within the area but nowhere more than on Questhaven Road. Multiple automobile accidents have occurred on this stretch of road, and the sheer amount is unusual. A former volunteer fire chief for the Elfin Forest said that "there are between sixteen and twenty car crashes every year here, and more times than not, they were blamed on the lady in white." When driving the area, please be careful; I do not believe that the White Witch does this on purpose.

There is another witch that stalks the Elfin Forest, and this one is anything but safe. Known as the Black Witch, this menacing hag is said to stem from the Gypsies who used to live in Harmony Grove. These Gypsies had been run out of the forest, and some of them were killed in the process.

Questhaven Road has so many accidents each year, many believe the White Witch of the forest is inadvertently causing them.

The original inhabitants of the forest were the Northern Diegueño Native People. It is said that when the Gypsies moved into the grove, they began to perform many rituals, one of which involved the summoning of deceased children. As the Natives were the only ones near, their dead children began walking the earth at the behest of the Gypsies. The white settlers began to see these children walking within their town and would hear them playing long into the night, keeping the townsfolk awake. When the villagers had had enough, they violently removed the Gypsies from the area. It is said that the Black Witch was one of the Gypsy priestesses who cursed the townsfolk and the entire forest, then killed herself to complete the ritual of the curse.

From the moment the Gypsy cursed the forest, people have reported seeing a woman dressed all in black, sometimes riding a large black horse. It is said that if she sees you, she will magically mark you for death and not stop until the deed is done. All she needs to do is make eye contact with her prey, and the person will drop dead from fright. Even today, there are tales from hikers and picnickers of seeing this black-clad woman and having one in their party begin screaming with fear while running away in abject terror. This specter has been known to cause insanity in some of those who have witnessed her. The Black Witch has marked herself as guardian of the forest, and woe to the trespasser if she should happen upon them.

The White Witch and her adversary, the Black Witch, are said to battle within the dark recesses of the Elfin Forest.

With the Gypsies summoning the children of the Diegueño and having been run out of the area, these poor children were never released from their bond to the living earth. As such, these waifs are still seen and heard in the forest to this day. It is not unusual for those visiting the Elfin Forest to go looking for what they believe to be lost children. There are times when these kids will call out to folks, beckoning them forward, only for the beguiled to find no one there when they get to where they believe the children to be. Oftentimes these folks will catch a fleeting glimpse of the kids just before the children fade into nothingness with the sound of a childish giggle. It is said that the Native children are lost and want the attention of those they hope can show them the way back to their loved ones.

There are other reports of folks seeing strange lights floating among the trees, the sounds of whispers from deep in the foliage and an eerie wind that comes from nowhere and is gone as quickly as it came. There are even reports of a dapper English gentleman who is seen sporting a topper and a walking stick and swinging a lantern. Who this fine gentleman may be no one knows, nor why he might be roaming the Elfin Forest in his afterlife.

Urban legends, fairy tales or the lost souls of those who have gone before us, I must leave up to my intrepid readers. The Elfin Forest is a beautiful mystery waiting for the plucky ParaTraveler to discover and explore. When trekking through this fantasy realm, keep an eye out for lost children and the White Witch, and if you see a lady in black atop a fine black steed, don't look at her and head in the opposite direction, just in case.

26

THE WHALEY HOUSE

No book about haunted Southern California could be complete without the Whaley House in the city of San Diego. This house has been known as the most haunted house in all of the country, and an urban legend has grown up about it being designated as such by Congress. This is just a myth but a fun one to consider. Even if it doesn't have the government's designation, this house has had so many reports about paranormal happenings within its walls that one would be hard-pressed to deny it is truly haunted.

The house was built by Thomas Whaley in 1855, directly over the spot where the brutal hanging of James "Yankee Jim" Robinson took place while Thomas watched. Yankee Jim suffered horribly for a crime that should have only given him a year or two in jail, and then the hanging itself was botched with Jim choking to death in a horrific manner. After Thomas and his wife, Anna, moved in, they knew that Yankee Jim had moved in as well. The Whaley family lived in the house for generations, and it is one of the best museums on the West Coast. Visitors will learn about not only the Whaleys but also what it must have been like to live in the birthplace of California in those early days—not to mention a chance to visit with the spirits that still reside here.

It was not long after the Whaleys moved into their new home that Anna began hearing footsteps and feeling as if she was being watched, even though she knew she was alone in the room. As her husband was oftentimes away from home and her sons were much too young to walk,

Many say that the Whaley House in Old Town San Diego is the most haunted house in America.

Anna worried that an intruder might be trying to rob them. Thomas also began to notice these disturbances and would comment to his friends and colleagues that he believed it was the spirit of Yankee Jim. Even though Thomas was not directly responsible for Jim's execution, Thomas always felt a pang of remorse over not trying to stop the brutal hanging. This, coupled with the fact the hanging took place where his home's archway now stood convinced both Thomas and Anna that it was indeed Robinson haunting their home.

Over the years, folks touring the home have claimed they were being watched from the stairway that leads up to the second floor. Others have said they were pushed as they descended these same steps, and the reports always concern the same step. Luckily, no one has been seriously hurt after being pushed; the spirit believed to be responsible for this is thought to be Yankee Jim. As Robinson has never been known for violent outbursts, it is not known why he would suddenly begin after the museum opened. Another theory regarding this spirit is that it may actually be a man by the name of Thomas Tanner. Tanner was an actor who died in an upstairs bedroom after performing in a show. This is just one possibility; unfortunately, we may never actually know the truth of who this culprit might be.

Folks walking through the home have sometimes reported hearing the sound of a baby crying in the upstairs bedroom, which was once the nursery for the family. It was here the couple's young son, Thomas Whaley Jr., passed away from scarlet fever at the age of eighteenth months. Scarlet fever can be a long, slow and painful way to die, and these cries may be the mournful suffering of young Tommy. Folks who have snapped photos in this same room have found the image of a baby will mysteriously appear in the pictures even though there was no child anywhere near the room or even in the home at the time the photo was taken. Many people believe that Thomas Jr.'s sudden and painful death possibly caused the child to imprint his agony into the very walls of the home, allowing guests to get just a glimpse of his last moments of life. We all pray that this is nothing more than what is called a residual haunting and not the spirit of the child himself. Orbs, as controversial as they are, are found in abundance in photos and videos from the nursery.

In one of the upstairs rooms is the replica of the stage where the Tanner Troupe stage performers held their shows. There have been many reports from this room of people seeing shadows moving about on the stage, and folks have heard the sounds of people talking as if they were awaiting a show. As soon as the guest walks into the room, all of the conversation they had heard immediately stops, and the room is once again quiet. The shadow that is seen may be that of Tanner, who by all accounts was a consummate professional. It may very well be Tanner, still performing for a spectral audience, as the voices heard before entering the theater might suggest. There are also reports from both guests and staff of hearing sounds of backstage commotion. These noises are coming from the area behind the stage, which is completely closed off to guests. Lights have also been known to turn on and off inside the theater room, and the door once leading into the nursery will mysteriously open and close. It sometimes rattles while people are sitting quietly staring at the stage.

Anna Whaley has stayed in her home since she passed away, and she is often seen strolling through her gardens. On quite a few occasions, visitors sitting or strolling through have mentioned talking to a lady, dressed in period garb, whom they believe is a docent. This woman will tell them about life at the house and the importance of family. This kindly lady is believed to be the spirit of Mrs. Whaley herself. Anna is also seen in the downstairs parlor, often sitting at the piano, an instrument she is known to favor. Later in life, Anna had a bedroom set up at the rear of the home on the ground floor overlooking the gardens she loved. This is where she passed away in 1913 at the age of eighty-one. While investigating the Whaley House, I

Above: These coins are set in the sidewalks and streets of Old Town to mark where bodies remain after their headstones were removed.

Right: This arch inside the Whaley Home is where James "Yankee Jim" Robinson was lynched by legal means.

performed what is commonly called an EVP session in the bedroom where Anna Whaley spent her final days looking out of the window at her garden. I asked Anna if she died while looking at her garden, and I recorded a distinct and clear response: "Yes, I so love my garden." It would seem that Anna is still enjoying her home long after her death. Anna is most often seen looking out one of the upstairs windows. What the Whaley matriarch is looking for no one knows—she could just be enjoying the view. When strolling past the home, keep an eye out for her. Anna Whaley is one of the most prolific spirits to reside in the home. She is sensed and seen so often, she even appeared to Regis Philbin during a filming regarding the spirits of the house.

There are other reports from both docents and guests that pillows and beds suddenly look as if someone has lain down and gone to sleep. Footsteps have been heard in empty rooms and following folks up the stairs, and people have heard faint moaning in the parlor, along with the sound of children laughing in the bedrooms. The garden has also been known as a place where children can be heard in playful merriment when there are no children present. Even the family's terrier dog has made an appearance in the home.

We know that Thomas Whaley is still looking after the family estate and often makes himself known by the strong smell of his cigar. The sweet stench of his cigar can be detected in almost every room of the house when Thomas shows up, and it is sometimes hard to tell where he is. There is a strict no smoking policy in California and the Whaley Museum, so it is easy to tell when Thomas is about. When Thomas is glimpsed, mostly upstairs or in the courtroom, he is usually dressed in the refinements of a man of his station, wearing a long coat and wide-brimmed hat. Thomas likes to move chairs around in the courtroom; this drives the docents wild because they will arrange the chairs in the proper order and find them moved around when they come back to check on the room.

There is an urban legend that has grown with each retelling about the spirit of a young girl seen running around the garden in the backyard. I say urban legend because that is what this story seems to be. The story goes that a friend of the Whaley children by the name of Annabelle Washburn was playing in the yard with the other kids and ran headlong into a clothesline. She was strangled to death before anyone could save her. This story has persisted for many years and has become one of the most told stories, outside of Yankee Jim, about the hauntings at the Whaley House. The trouble is it most likely never happened. No record has ever been found of a child or family by this name living in the area near Old Town San

Diego, and no death certificates or newspaper reports were filed, which would have been written if a death at such a prominent family's home had occurred. In fact, there is no historical record of any kind that has ever surfaced to support this story.

Urban legends aside, it is hard to think that the Whaley House is simply a mundane museum in the heart of one of the most haunted sections of one of the most haunted cities in the country. I was a skeptic of the Whaley haunts, the house and the family, but they decided to prove me wrong and force me to believe the many tales of one of the most haunted houses in America.

27
VALLECITO STAGE STOP

Out in the desert of eastern San Diego County sits a tiny cemetery surrounded by campsites and a replica of an old stage stop. Not many folks know about this little place—maybe because it is in a remote, inhospitable region or perhaps because many people don't look at the Southern California desert as a place to spend a weekend outdoors in a tent. This little cemetery in the middle of nowhere is occupied by no more than three graves, and at least one of the occupants is not content to stay in her plot. For those spending the night in one of the many campsites, keep your eyes and ears open for the tell-tale clop of horses, the commands of a stage driver and the soft footfalls of the Lady in White. For you see, the old Vallecito stage stop may be the most haunted campground in California.

When gold was discovered at Sutter's Mill in Northern California in 1849, prospectors and immigrants began arriving in large numbers to seek their fortunes. Many of them used the southern route from Texas, in what came to be known as "the journey of death," and Vallecito became one of the main places to rest and get ready for the final leg of their trek. This road was the only route into Southern California and followed the same route taken by Juan Bautista de Anza in 1775, who had been coming from Tucson to the California missions. It has been said that upward of two hundred wagons at one time would camp at Vallecito Springs.

James Lassitor moved to Vallecito in 1853 and saw a business opportunity in the many travelers passing through. Enlarging the existing warehouse, he moved his wife and three kids into the improved adobe building. Lassitor

The Stage Stop at Vallecito may be a replica, but that hasn't stopped the spirits from remaining at the once busy location.

began feeding and housing those arriving on the stage, and it wasn't long before he knew the opportunity he had envisioned was indeed a good one. Then, when the federal government helped establish the Butterfield Stage and stops, Vallecito became a "home stop" along the famous stage route. A home stop was where passengers could get out and receive a hot meal and a night's stay, which were unavailable at the other stage stops. Once the Butterfield Stage Company arrived, guests began arriving almost every day, most heading for the northern gold fields, others waiting for their loved ones to arrive for a new start in the warm climes of sunny California. One of these, a beautiful young woman, may have never left and is still waiting for her beloved to arrive so they can start their lives together or, at least, their afterlives.

Perhaps the most famous ghost story at the old stage stop is that of the White Lady of Vallecito. Engaged to be married, her fiancé wanted to make sure he had the means to support his new wife. Having traveled to the gold fields of California without his love, he told her that he would send for her when he had found his fortune. A year after her betrothed had left, she received a letter telling her to come to Sacramento, where they would be married. The woman, some say her name was Eileen O'Conner, booked passage on the stage and headed out to begin her new life. Unfortunately, just before reaching the Vallecito stop, she became deathly ill. She had to be carried into the station and was placed in a bed in the rear room, where the agents at the stop took care of her for days. Frail and sick, she died from her illness. Going through her luggage, they found her wedding dress and buried her in it. She is one of only three people buried at the Campo Santo Cemetery next to the station; as the station attendants did not know the woman's name, she was placed in an unmarked grave between the only two headstones within the cemetery.

It is said that those staying in the camping area will see this sad apparition still walking the grounds as if in search of something or someone. It is believed that she hopes her beloved husband-to-be will arrive to claim her hand so the two can be together in eternity. It is said that some spirits can never rest in an unmarked grave; this could be the reason why this lost young lady cannot find peace in death. If a ParaTraveler sees this lost soul while visiting Vallecito, please be kind to the spirit and let her know it is OK to move on and that her beloved waits for her on the other side.

The White Lady of Vallecito is not the only spirit at the stage stop with this sort of moniker; this area of the southeastern desert also has the ghost known as the White Horse of Vallecito. It would seem that once upon a time, four robbers held up a stage on its way east. The driver handed over the money box without a fight; however, as the bandits rode away, the driver drew his rifle and fired on the four men. One of the thieves dropped to the ground while the others made a fast getaway. As the stage driver neared the fallen man, he was amazed to find two bandits lying in the sand: the one he had shot and one who had obviously been killed with a pistol. Seeing this, he realized that the other two robbers were making sure their share of the loot would be larger than originally planned. The other two crooks continued on to Vallecito but buried the gold in the desert before they arrived to throw off suspicion that they were the thieves. As is the way with greedy men, they began to argue while eating their dinner at Vallecito. One of the men, seemingly fed up with the dispute, got up, saying he would resume the "discussion" when he returned and then left the building. A few minutes later, the door burst open, and there, riding his beautiful white stallion, the other bandit rode into the stage stop and shot his partner. As he turned to flee, the dying man, in one last moment of defiance, pulled his gun and shot the last bandit in the back, killing him instantly. The sound of the gun, and the dead man pulling on the reins as he fell, frightened the horse, which bolted and ran on into the desert and the night. It is said that the horse still roams the area where the thieves buried their ill-gotten gold.

There are treasure seekers who know the story of the bandits and will go out into the surrounding desert looking for the buried treasure; many of them come back with tales of seeing the White Horse of Vallecito. For some, this is a good omen that they are digging in the right area, and they will go back many times looking for the gold; for others. the sight of this spectral horse has scared them so badly that they can never bring themselves to go back. Still, other fortune questers have reported seeing what they claim are two cowboys watching them from a distance; they say these specters stare at them while they dig and only go away once the digging has stopped. Many believe these cowboys are in fact the ghosts of the bandits who killed each other after burying their loot to make sure no one else finds it and steals their cache from them. One can only wonder what they will do if it is ever actually found.

Another legend that surrounds the old Vallecito stage stop is that of a phantom stagecoach that can be seen and heard, usually late at night. It pauses briefly at the Vallecito stage stop and then, continuing on, always vanishes from sight as it gets near the edge of the roadway. The tale told is

Only three graves are located in the tiny cemetery; one of these is a bride who still waits for her love to arrive so they can finally be married.

that this stage was carrying a box of gold from El Paso to the city of San Diego. While in Yuma, Arizona, the stage guard became ill, and the driver, knowing the schedule was tight, went on without him. Somewhere near the Carrizo Wash and the nearby Vallecito Station, the stage was held up by bandits, the driver was killed and the chest of gold was stolen. In an odd twist of fate, the four mules continued on with the body of their driver dead in his seat with the reins still held in his dead hands. The stage disappeared into the desert, never to be seen again—that is, until it began to appear as a spectral carriage forever roaming the Anza Borrego Desert. Many folks who have spent the night at Vallecito Campground have reported waking up at night to the sound of horses and hearing the wheels of the stagecoach. A few have said they panicked as they looked out of their tent or RV to see a full horse-drawn stagecoach bearing down on them, only to find it passes right through and continues on its way once past them. Many of these folks, thinking it is just a dream or nightmare, go back to sleep and think nothing more about it until they wake up the next morning to find wagon wheel tracks right where they had "dreamed" of seeing the phantom carriage heading toward them. They even see the tracks stop just at the edge of their tent, only to begin again on the other side.

Vallecito Stage Stop and campground may be in a remote area of eastern San Diego, but one cannot dispute the beauty of the area or its historical importance to the growth and development of California. The Anza Borrego has many tales of spirits, lost gold and phantom sailing ships, enough to fill a book all on its own, but Vallecito may be the one place in the entire desert where you will find stories of lost love, missing gold, murder and banditry all rolled up in one small place. Vallecito is a definite must stop on any ParaTravelers list of places to visit.

EPILOGUE

Southern California is a place many folks from around the world visit for vacation, to see their favorite movie stars and hopefully catch a glimpse of a public film shoot. They come to tour a real working movie studio and become amazed at the movie magic of the same studios attractions in their amusement park. Folks come to see a famous mouse, marvel at the rides of fantasy and gape as they see their favorite childhood characters come to life before their eyes. They bask in the sunshine, their toes in the warm beach sand, and snack on corn dogs, churros and street tacos. Folks come for the scenery and never realize that there is a whole world surrounding them—one much duller and much darker than the one of the living.

One never sees the phantom grips and crew still working the movie sets; they never see the long-dead but still devoted movie stars even now plying their art or those that have come back to continue riding the attractions for eternity. Obscured by the laughter of children and the smiles of the young are those who still ride in fantasy the dark rides and rollercoasters the mouse has gifted us or the man who still smiles at the families to whom he has brought so much joy. But for those who still sail on a now stationary liner, the kids and seekers of eternal fun or those who went too soon, along with those who are still keeping the history of Southern California alive by their ceaseless devotion, even after death, we owe it to them, even if we cannot see them, to at least remember them.

BIBLIOGRAPHY

AMARGOSA HOTEL

Amargosa Opera House. http://www.amargosaoperahouse.org.
Legends of America. "Death Valley Junction & the Haunted Amargosa
Hotel." https://www.legendsofamerica.com.

BOOKS

Clune, Brian. *Hollywood Obscura*. Atglen, PA: Schiffer Books, 2017.
Clune, Brian, and Bob Davis. *California's Historic Haunts*. Atglen, PA: Schiffer
Books, 2014.
———. *Ghosts and Legends of Calico*. Charleston, SC: The History Press, 2020.
———. *Ghosts of the Queen Mary*. Charleston, SC: The History Press, 2014.

DISNEYLAND

Haunted Orange County. "Haunted Disney Stories." https://hauntedoc.com.
World History. "History of Disneyland." May 21, 2017. https://worldhistory.us.

Bibliography

Elfin Forest

Hidden San Diego. "Elfin Forest." https://hiddensandiego.net.
Mysterious Universe. "The Haunted Elfin Forest of San Diego County."
   https://mysteriousuniverse.org.

Glen Tavern

Glen Tavern Inn. "History." https://www.glentavern.com.
Hughes, Bill. "Glen Tavern Inn." *Los Angeles Times*, December 21, 1986.
   https://www.latimes.com.

Las Cruces Adobe

Santa Maria Times. "Judith Dale: Las Cruses—The Forgotten Crossroads."
   May 9, 2020. https://santamariatimes.com.
Weird California. "Las Cruces Adobe." http://www.weirdca.com.

The Los Angeles Arboretum

The Arboretum. "Our History." https://www.arboretum.org.
Weird California. "LA County Arboretum." http://www.weirdca.com.

Majestic/Ventura Theater

Bennett, Miles. "Nightmare on Main Street: The 'Hauntings' of Ventura."
   Cougar Press, October 16, 2018. https://thecougarpress.org.
Gregory, Kim Lamb. "Ghost Hunters Describe Some of Ventura County's
   Haunted Places." VC Star. https://archive.vcstar.com.

Special thanks to the manager of the theater, Stefan Brigati, for sending me the history and proofing the chapter. Thank you, my friend. Did I mention Stefan is a fantastic musician and performer?

BIBLIOGRAPHY

SAN JUAN CAPISTRANO

Cuniff, Meghann M. "Spooky Stories Still Haunt Historic San Juan Capistrano." *Orange County Register*, October 31, 2013. https://www.ocregister.com.

SANTA MARIA INN

Haunted Rooms of America. "The Historic Santa Maria Inn." https://www.hauntedrooms.com.

Rose, Rebecca. "A Century of Stories: Santa Maria Inn Celebrates 100 Years." *Santa Maria Sun*, May 10, 2017. http://www.santamariasun.com.

ZALUD HOUSE

National Register of Historic Places Nomination Form. "Zalud House." https://npgallery.nps.gov.

Welles, Darla. "Pearle Zalud: Lady of the House Still Giving." *Porterville Record*, March 5, 2002. https://www.recorderonline.com.

Wray, James. "Ghost Adventures Investigate the Zalud House in Porterville." Monsters & Critics, December 10, 2016. https://www.monstersandcritics.com.

Special thanks go to Zalud House curator Heather Raymond-Huerta for giving me a great history of both the Zalud House and its many haunts.

ABOUT THE AUTHOR

Brian Clune is the co-founder and the historian for Planet Paranormal Radio and Planet Paranormal Investigations. He has traveled the entire state of California researching its haunted hot spots and historical locations in an effort to bring knowledge of the paranormal and the wonderful history of the state to those interested in learning.

His interest in history has led him to volunteer aboard the USS *Iowa* and the Fort MacArthur Military Museum as well as giving lectures at colleges and universities around the state. He has been involved with numerous TV shows, including *Ghost Adventures*, *My Ghost Story*, *Dead Files* and *Ghost Hunters* and was the subject in a companion documentary for the movie *Paranormal Asylum*. He has also appeared on numerous local and national and international radio programs. Clune is the co-host for the radio program *The Full Spectrum Project*, which deals in subjects ranging from ghosts and murders to all things odd and weird both natural and supernatural.

His other books include *California's Historic Haunts*, published by Schiffer Books, and the highly acclaimed *Ghosts of the Queen Mary*, published by The History Press, as well as *Ghosts and Legends of Alcatraz* and *Ghosts and Legends of Calico*, all with coauthor Bob Davis. Brian and Bob also teamed up to write the riveting biography of Ghost Box creator Frank Sumption. Clune is also the author of *Haunted San Pedro* and *Hollywood Obscura*, the spellbinding book dealing with Hollywood's dark and sordid tales of murder and ghosts. Clune is currently working on other titles for The History Press and is teaching courses in paranormal studies at California State University Dominguez Hills.

Clune lives in Southern California with his loving wife, Terri, his three wonderful children and of course, Wandering Wyatt!

Visit us at
www.historypress.com